change to
point
1 our
starts.

D0433974

# Routledge Popular Music

*A series of books for schools edited by* Graham Vulliamy and Edward Lee

# Edward Lee

**Routledge & Kegan Paul**
London, Boston, Melbourne and Henley

First published in 1982
by Routledge & Kegan Paul Ltd
39 Store Street, London WC1E 7DD
9 Park Street, Boston, Mass. 02108, USA
296 Beaconsfield Parade, Middle Park,
Melbourne, 3206, Australia and
Broadway House, Newtown Road,
Henley-on-Thames, Oxon RG9 1EN
Set in 11/14pt Helvetica by Input Typesetting Ltd, London
and printed in Great Britain by St Edmundsbury Press
Bury St Edmunds, Suffolk
© Edward Lee, 1982

ISBN 0–7100–0902–X

# Contents

# Preface

Have you ever asked an old person 'What was it like when you were young?' Or wondered what sort of people built an ancient building, or how they lived? Have you ever wondered where your family came from, and what sort of people your great-great-grandparents were?

This book can't give the answers to those questions, of course. But it does set out to tell you something about the music which those people, your ancestors, liked. The music they danced to, the songs that made them laugh, the songs in which they expressed their sadness.

Nowadays we have pop music. And before that – of course – there were the Beatles, Elvis Presley, and many others. And before that, when your grandfather was young? Bing Crosby, Paul Whiteman, and others – music from America.

But what did your grandfather's grandfather listen to, in the days before the motorcar, when Victoria was Queen of England, and when America had not long ceased to be a British colony?

That is the subject of this book: popular music before the American invasion – the music of the village green, the drawing room, and the music hall.

'Popular music is functional' (see pp. 49–50). Contrast this picture by Hogarth with that of a classical audience (see p. 51)

# Introduction

## Popular taste in the nineteenth century

Nowadays we often hear people complain about how fast life is changing, compared with how slowly things altered in days gone by. Perhaps the pace of life really is faster; but a man who lived a century or more ago would have been amazed if you had told him he was living in a peaceful, slow-moving time. More than likely he would have pointed out that he lived in a rapidly growing modern city, with new inventions being made almost daily. Yet his parents still lived in a village which had remained unchanged for hundreds of years, where people spoke a dialect so strange that only those born locally could understand it. To come from a medieval village to a modern industrial town with factories and trains – 'If that is not rapid change, what is?' he would have said.

In the nineteenth century there was a great variety in the ways in which people lived; this was reflected in their music, and one aim of this book is to show that variety. But let's begin by putting some shape into the story.

1 Music differed according to area – the music of Scotland was not the same as that of southern England, for example.
2 Music differed according to social class – manual

labourers did not have the same tastes as bank clerks.

3 Music differed from town to country.

We shall explore all these differences in this book. But before doing so, there are a few more points to be made.

This book is concerned with popular music. For us this means 'any music which is the taste of the majority of people, or at least of a very large number of people.' Thus the music which you can hear today on Radio 3 is not popular music, because it is appreciated only by a minority of people. We shall call that type of music 'classical'.

Finally, you need to be clear that before 1914 (the start of the First World War) there were basically two sorts of popular music: the popular music of the town (which we can call 'urban' or 'city' music), and the traditional popular music of the countryside, which we call 'folk' music, and which will be our first topic.

# 1 Folk music
## the music of the countryside

**Folk music in the English countryside**

Until about 1750, the way of life of people living in the English countryside was much the same as it had been in the Middle Ages. When change did take place, it did so very slowly. So it is not surprising that the music which country people loved changed equally slowly. We know, for example, that in the sixteenth century there was a dance tune called 'Quodling's Delight'. In 1650 the same tune appeared in a collection of dance music under the name 'Goddesses'. A hundred years later still it was taken a little slower and sung; we still know this version as 'The Oak and the Ash' ('A North country maid/Up to London had strayed . . .').

### Work songs

Country people were mostly agricultural workers on farms or big estates, or they offered skilled services, such as those of the blacksmith or wheelwright. They worked very long hours. Many people got up before it was light, worked all day, and only stopped at dusk. Domestic servants would often work until the master of the house had gone to bed, even when this meant that they were up until midnight or later.

Since work was such an important part of life, it is not surprising that people made up songs about it. Often these told of the hard conditions:

# 2 The music of the countryside

*opposite*
Weighing anchor
at the start of the
voyage to lay the
first Transatlantic
Telegraph line.
Fiddle music
makes working
the capstan
easier

In my old mother's days, as I understand,
There were twenty pounds wages and a guinea in
  hand:
But now the poor servants, they are so brought
  down,
They scarcely can get ten pounds and a crown.

Men who lived near the sea coast often worked on ships, naturally enough. These were sailing ships, and there was a lot of heavy work to be done, especially the setting of the sails and the lifting of the anchor. Singing made this work easier.

The singing was led by a shantyman. He would sing out the story, and the men would join in the chorus (this type of singing is called the 'call-and-response form', and occurs a lot in blues and similar music). The well-known shanty 'Blow the Man Down' is built up in this manner:

*Shantyman*:  They gave me three months in
  Liverpool Town,
*Chorus*:  To me way-ay, blow the man down,
*Shantyman*:  For kicking this policeman, blowing
  him down.
*Chorus*:  Give us some time to blow the man
  down.

Another important type of work song was the street cry, which was to be heard wherever tradesmen walked the streets advertising their services. People born before the First World War can often still remember the beautiful song of the lavender seller:

Who will buy my sweet lavender,
Gathered at the break of day?

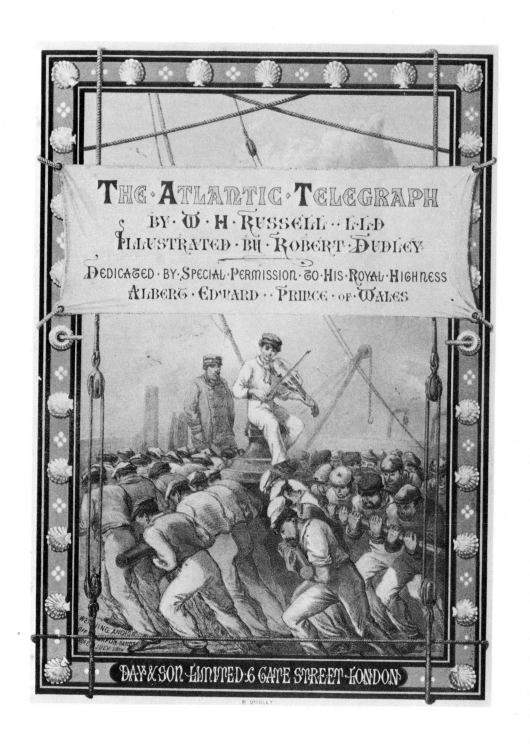

A London street cry – the call of the orange and lemon seller

### News songs

Though there was no radio or television in those days, people liked to hear the news of great events and strange happenings, just as they do today.

Until about 1860 an important way in which news was spread was by means of the ballad. Ballads were long songs, which sometimes told fictional stories, and sometimes gave accounts of true events. They were spread by ballad sellers, who travelled the country singing for money and selling printed copies of the words of their songs. These copies were called broadsides, and usually cost either a halfpenny or a penny a sheet. The ballads, like today's newspapers, could be very critical of those in power, who in turn did not hesitate to punish the ballad maker in ways which would be impossible today: for example, an offender could be imprisoned, whipped, or have his ears cut off.

**Ritual songs**

In the countryside, in times gone by, there were many important festivals, which people looked forward to as a change from their hard daily lives. Among these festivals were New Year, Plough Monday, Shrove Tuesday, Easter Day, May Day, Whitsuntude, Midsummer Eve, Halloween and, of course, Christmas. Some of the festivals were Christian feast days, but all of them had important links with the changes of the seasons and the growing of the crops. For example, there had been a festival in mid-December long before the birth of Christ, to celebrate the arrival of the shortest day, when men could begin to look forward to the end of the winter. Originally such times were celebrated with pagan magical ceremonies.

A ceremony which is carried out in exactly the same way every year is known as a ritual, and most rituals involve music. One such ritual took place on Boxing Day, when people went into the woods to hunt the wren. This explains the strange nature of the words of the well-known folksong 'The Cutty Wren':

'O where are you going?' said Milder to Malder,
'O we may not tell you' said Festle to Fose,
'We're off to the woods' said John the Red Nose,
'We're off to the woods' said John the Red Nose.

Another important festival was May Day. This used to be seen as the first day of summer, and therefore a time for great celebration. It was the custom for young people to go out to the woods to collect May branches to decorate the houses and church on May Eve (30 April). Then on May Day there would be feasting and dancing round the Maypole. There were many complaints that the young people got out of hand, and misbehaved. The sixteenth-century Puritan Philip Stubbes wrote that 'On the eve of May . . . of forty, three score or a hundred maids going to the wood overnight, there have been scarcely the third part of them returned home again undefiled.'

**Religious songs**
Since 1914 things have changed incredibly in certain ways. It is, for example, uncommon for a person to be a regular churchgoer these days, even though many people might still claim to have a religious belief. However, it was a very different matter in centuries gone by. Almost everyone was a member of one church or another, and at many times in history there was a great deal of pressure upon people to attend church regularly. In Victorian times this was largely achieved by the fact that your family and friends would have been critical if you had been absent from church too often. But in the time of Queen Elizabeth I, for example, you could actually

The Abbots Bromley Horn Dance is a unique survival of ancient ritual dancing

be fined for failing to attend the Sunday morning service without good reason.

In church, special religious music was performed, as is still true today. However, until the eighteenth century this music was made for people by the clergy or a choir, rather than sung by the congregation. (This was not so in Nonconformist churches, where everyone did join in, though the music was for a long time restricted to the chanting of the Psalms.)

Outside the church, though, people made up songs of their own to express their religious beliefs. One example, which is still popular, is the 'Cherry Tree Carol', which tells of Joseph's suspicions when Mary is found to be carrying a child. Today this might well seem a surprising subject for a religious song –

we have tended to become so respectful towards religion that Jesus and his parents are often no longer seen as having been real people, with feelings like our own. In earlier times people appreciated this fact much more, and in the strength of their religious feelings liked to imagine in detail what it must have been like to live through the Bible events. Seen from this point of view, what was more natural than that Joseph should have been suspicious of the pregnancy of his virgin wife?

## Songs of adventure and mystery

It was mentioned above that the ballad not only dealt with news but also with imaginary events. This was important to our ancestors because it answered a very deep human need.

One of the main tasks of television today is to entertain. It presents plays about people both of today, and in history. It can show us distant places and events; with the tricks of the camera, it can even work magic for us. None of this was possible, of course, hundreds of years ago. Yet men still had imaginations, and a need to satisfy them. The ballad helped to do this, since it was concerned with romance and adventure, violence, love, and especially magic. The ballads are too long to quote here, but you may already have come across those written about Robin Hood, for instance.

The ballads had another use, which was to provide a brief escape for those whose daily lives were very hard. Throughout the centuries, an important purpose of some popular art has been 'wish fulfilment', that is, to give people in a story the happy ending which they know cannot happen in real life. Perhaps the most famous example of this type of story is that of Cinderella. Sometimes, though, the story was romantic but sad. So it is not surprising that one ballad which was very popular was that of a handsome knight and his true love, entitled 'Lord Lovell'. It begins:

Lord Lovell stood at his castle gate,
Calming his milk-white steed,
When up came Lady Nancy Bell,
To wish her lover 'God Speed'.

The story ends unhappily. Lady Nancy dies, and Lord Lovell, having discovered this on his return, dies of sorrow. But the lovers remain true, even in death:

And they buried her in the chancel high,
And they buried him in the choir;
And out of her grave sprung a red, red rose,
And out of his sprung a briar.

And they grew till they grew to the church roof,
And then they couldn't grow any higher,
So they twined themselves into a true lovers' knot
For all lovers true to admire.

## Love songs

In all ages a very large number of songs are written about some aspect of love between men and women. Many of these songs are short in length and express the singer's emotions. They are called *lyrics* to distinguish them from the other main type of folk song, the ballad, which is a long song that tells a story. In folk music there are many love songs which, though simple in language, express feelings in an effective and sensitive way:

I must be going, no longer staying,
The burning Thames I have to cross.
O, I must be guided without a stumble
Into the arms of my dear lass.

A notable difference between many modern songs and those of folk music lies in their treatment of sexual matters. Though it is true to say that in the past ten years pop music has become much more free in this respect, before then there was nothing like the direct and frank approach of this folk lyric:

I wish, I wish, but it's all in vain,
I wish I were a maid again.
But a maid again I shall never be,
Till apples grow on an orange tree.

I wish my baby it was born,
And smiling on its papa's knee,
And I to be in yon churchyard
With the long green grass growing over me.

When my apron strings hung low,
He followed me through frost and snow.
But now my apron's to my chin,
He passes by and says nothing.

### Voices and instruments in folk music

So far we have learned something of the subjects which folk music dealt with, and the two main types of song (the ballad and the lyric) which it used for the purpose. It is now time to consider the way in which the music was performed.

Traditional English folk music was performed mostly by men. Women sang when working, or in the home, but they did not normally sing publicly. When performing, the singer would usually stand, making little movement, and often with the eyes closed. The sound was described as 'a pure stream of melody' by the folksong collector Cecil Sharp. It was customary to speak (rather than sing) the last line of the song after the song was finished, as a way of rounding off. The tune would vary a little from performance to performance, especially as singers would 'ornament' the tune, that is, they would add little trills and decorations.

Folk instruments had to be cheap, portable and loud. Wherever possible they were home-made. Probably the earliest instrument was the drum. Often it was used together with a form of penny whistle; the combination was known as the pipe and tabor.

It often comes as a surprise to English people to learn that the bagpipe was also an English folk instrument, which only fell into disuse in the eighteenth century. It was a simpler instrument than the Scottish pipe we know today, and could be constructed fairly easily from simple materials – some wood and a sheep's stomach. It was always seen as a 'low' instrument, and was associated with dancing and drunkenness.

From about 1600 onwards the violin became very popular. It is strange to us to think that it was originally regarded as a crude instrument, fit only to be played in taverns, in contrast to the viol favoured by the well-to-do. It is worth noting that folk fiddlers tend to approach the technique of playing the instrument differently from classically trained players.

Morris dancers (see pp. 120–3) preferred the concertina, an instrument which became popular in the nineteenth century. It makes a sweet and jaunty sound, and ought to be more popular than it is today.

The important point about the use of instruments in English folk music is that, unlike symphonic musicians, the performers did not rely on a particular set of instruments. They used whatever they could get hold of, and in any combination that took their fancy. The sound of the music is therefore very different from that of a symphony orchestra. This fact

*over page left* Folk instruments: the performer fingers the pipe with one hand and beats a rhythm on the tabor with the other; *right* the concertina: the player makes notes by pressing buttons, not, as on the piano accordion, with keys

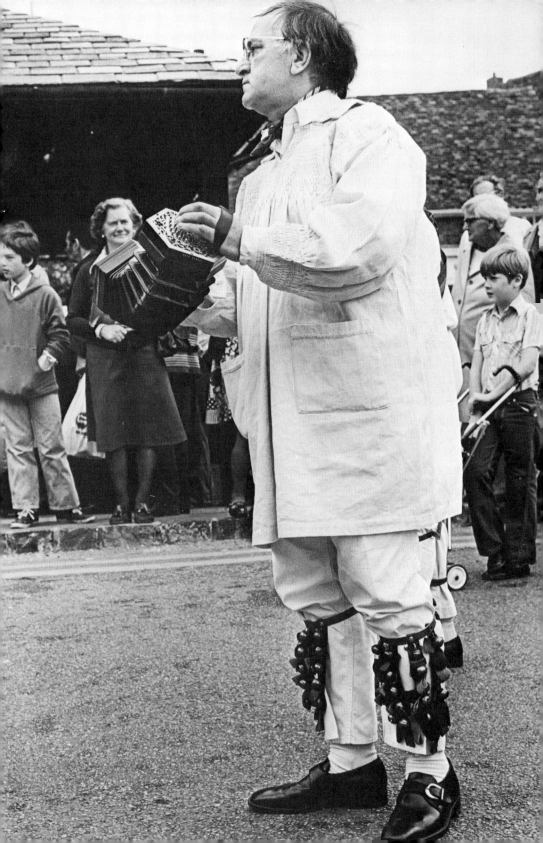

has meant that this ancient music is still enjoyed by many listeners today, since our modern taste is for new and exciting combinations of sound – many a pop record has been made a success by using an unusual blend of instruments.

## Folk music in the British Isles

The music discussed in the previous pages was that of the south of England. In many ways the traditional picture of this part of the country is correct – it really was an agricultural region, with thatched cottages and apple orchards. It was a very important part of the country because it contained the capital, London, the nearest ports to the Continent, the first universities (Oxford and Cambridge) and the best farm land.

What has been said about the music of this region is in some ways true of all British folk music; every area had songs for work, about love, and topical events, as well as ritual and religious songs.

But every area of Britain had some distinctive qualities; in some ways music differed greatly from region to region.

### North-east England

For instance, other parts of England also had their own music, form of speech and customs, which are very interesting. One of the most distinctive areas, and the richest in folk music, was the north-east. 'Geordie' is still a very different accent, and the people who live in the north-east are very proud of their region. Much of this is due to the fact that for a long time the two most important forms of work were mining and fishing. These are both hard and dangerous jobs, in which a man must be tough and reliable, but jobs which he can be proud to do. It is not therefore surprising that some of the finest north-eastern songs were about terrible pit disasters. A famous example of this type of song was made as recently as 1934; it is called 'The Gresford Disaster'. It is very bitter about those who did not have to face the dangers of coal mining, yet took all the profits:

> The Lord Mayor of London's collecting,
> To help out both children and wives;
> The owners have sent some white lilies
> To pay for the poor colliers' lives.

Despite such tragedies, life was not all gloom for the people of the north-east. They could laugh about everyday life. In the song 'The Row upon the Stairs', for instance, two ladies argue about their duties in maintaining a tenement block:

> Says Mistress Bell to Mistress Todd
> 'Ye'd better clean the stairs!
> Y've missed your turn for many a week,
> The neighbours all did theirs!'

> Says Mistress Todd to Mistress Bell,
> 'I tell ye Mistress Bell,
> Ye'd better mind your own affairs,
> And clean the stairs yoursel'!'

## The Celtic countries

When we talk about 'Britain' we tend to think of one country. Yet in Britain there are four countries – England, Ireland, Scotland and Wales – each of which at one time had its own different language, music and customs. In a short book like this we cannot possibly study these countries in detail, though it would be very worth while to do so, since too many English people have very little idea of how their fellow-countrymen have thought, felt and made music for hundreds of years.

However, lack of space is not the only reason why we shall neglect the large amount of beautiful music which was made in these countries. The other reason is related to an important idea which this book hopes to put across. Briefly, it is that as industry grew during the Industrial Revolution, which took place roughly between 1750 and 1850, people poured into the cities in search of the jobs, bright lights and (for some) big rewards of the city. More important, they rarely went back home. As a result, the old traditions, including the old music, were soon abandoned and forgotten. It is hard to pipe in the New Year on a bagpipe when you are alone, or there is no piper. It is pointless and frustrating to speak Irish when no one else does. Furthermore, the old Celtic languages and customs were seen as inferior not only by the English, but even by upper-class people in the Celtic countries themselves. The old ways had to be put aside by anyone who wanted to get on. The change was forced along by the fact that for a very long time children who spoke a Celtic language as their first language were punished for doing so in school.

*Ireland*

It seems likely that Ireland was settled by Goidelic Celts in about 500 BC; thus the people originally spoke Irish, though few do so now as a native tongue. Ireland has always had some special difficulties, apart from those caused by the Industrial Revolution. First, it was and still is predominantly Roman Catholic in religion. Second, it was occupied by the English in the time of Henry II. This fact remains a source of bitter conflict even to the present day, and was made worse when England and Scotland became Protestant in the sixteenth century.

Nevertheless, much old Irish music survives and is still popular. The earliest Irish musicians were bards, that is professional poets and singers. Some of their stories of magic, monsters, and heroes such as Cuchulain and Brian Boru still exist.

Ireland is also famous for its dancing. Originally the dances were stately and fairly simple, and involved many people. One such was the 'rince fada', danced upon ceremonial occasions such as May Day, and the landing of the King in Ireland. But in the eighteenth century the Irish began to take an interest in step dances, such as the jig, in which one dancer tries his skill at complicated footwork.

At one time Ireland was famous for its harpists. The harp is still a national emblem, both officially, on Irish coins, and unofficially, on Guinness bottles. If you ever visit Dublin, you should see the oldest Irish harp that still exists; it is known as the 'Brian Boru' harp, and is in Trinity College Library.

In the eighteenth century traditional harp playing began to lose its popularity; soon the instrument was only being played by a few old men. Fortunately, some of the harp music was collected at a special festival held in Belfast in 1792, by a man called Edward Bunting. He was followed by other collectors of folk music, of whom the most famous were Thomas Moore (who made popular some of the most well-known Irish tunes, such as 'The Minstrel Boy' and 'The Last Rose of Summer') and Francis O'Neill. O'Neill was a folk flute player, who emigrated to the USA in search of work. There he began what became a collection of nearly two thousand folk pieces. He finally became the Chief of Police in Chicago, and, so great was his interest in music, that it was said that if you were an Irishman and knew some folk tunes, you were always certain of a job on

the police force!
  Recently, young Irish people have become very
interested in the American country and western style,

Turlough Carolan, the greatest player of the Irish harp, still influences folk musicians today. Like many other harpists, he was blind; music was one of the few things a blind man could do

and their groups now have names such as the Rocky Mountain Boys. But the sweetness of the tunes still remains very traditional, as does the content of the lyrics, which often speak of the feelings of a young man working abroad who remembers his girl back at home.

*Scotland*

Scottish music is divided into two types, according to area. The first type is Lowland music. This is music which has much in common with the folk music of England; for example, many of the ballads in the famous collection made by Francis Child are found in both Scotland and England. Lowland music also includes many songs which are typically Scottish in sound, but which have English words, and are known all over the world, such as 'Annie Laurie' and 'Auld Lang Syne'. Much of what we know about such songs is due to the work of folksong collectors, such as Robert Burns, James Hogg, Sir Walter Scott and William Motherwell. Burns also composed many fine lyrics for old tunes – the two songs mentioned above are examples.

Highland music is the other type of Scottish music, and was very different. This is because of the fact that Highland people have a different history to those of the Lowlands. Many are the descendants of settlers who went to Scotland over 1500 years ago. Many of these people still speak Scottish Gaelic, which is similar to Irish, and this, together with the fact that they live in very remote areas, has meant that the old traditions survived until very recently.

As in Ireland, there were many legends told in song. Until about 1600 these were passed on, as in Ireland, by bards. Learning to be a bard was a long and difficult business. Bards had to learn by heart over 330 different types of poetic rhythm. To do this they would spend the whole day in a darkened room, with the doors and windows shut, and wrapping their cloaks around their heads to aid concentration.

Highland funerals were also very different from those of England or the Lowlands. For example, there would be a professional mourning woman who 'followed the body, every now and then striking the coffin with her hands like a drum, and making all the din possible, and keeping time with the movements of the men.' Afterwards there would be much feasting and drinking (this was called a 'funeral wake'), and people would come from miles around to join in. Behaviour was very different from what we would expect today in such circumstances. Whisky was cheap and things could get very rowdy. One traveller, Mr John Pinkerton, wrote in 1772 that 'A wake continues till daylight, with such gambols and frolics among the younger part of the company, that the loss which occasioned them, is often more than supplied by the consequences of that night.'

The music was either sung, or played upon the harp or bagpipe. Later the fiddle became popular in all parts of Scotland as an accompaniment to the lively strathspeys and reels, which are still enjoyed both in Scotland and abroad.

The preservation of traditional folk music in Scotland (and also in Wales) was greatly affected by religious changes. In the sixteenth century, England, Scotland and Wales rejected the Roman Catholic faith and became Protestant. Later, Scotland and Wales turned to even newer and stricter forms of Protestant religion; there, religious beliefs were held more intensely than in England. So, for example, instruments are not used in the Church of Scotland;

Probably the most internationally known form of British folk music – Highland dancers and a bagpiper

there is therefore no organ, such as we associate with English services.

Though the Scottish Church was strict in all areas, it was nowhere more so than in the Highlands. An extract from an interview with a lady on the Isle of Lewis, in the Outer Hebrides, by folksong collector Alexander Carmichael, illustrates what happened:

*Woman*: The good men and the good ministers who arose did away with the songs and stories, the music and the dancing, the sports and games that were perverting the minds and ruining the souls of the people, leading them into folly and stumblings.

*Carmichael*: But how did the people themselves come to discard their sports and pastimes?

*Woman*: Oh, the good ministers and the good elders preached against them, and went among the people, and brought them to forsake their follies, and return to wisdom. They made the people break and burn their pipes and fiddles. If there was a foolish man here or there who demurred, the good ministers and the good elders themselves broke and burnt their instruments.

In this way, pressures at home combined with those from abroad mentioned earlier to destroy much of the ancient traditions of the Celtic peoples.

*Wales*

Wales is also a Celtic country, but it was occupied by another race of Celts, the Brythonic people. Its language is thus very different from that of Scotland and Ireland. However, as in the other Celtic lands, the bard was very important. We know a fair amount about Welsh bards, since in 942 AD Prince Hywel Dda set down laws about their profession. We even have such detail as the fact that 'When the queen shall will to hear a song in her chamber, let the bard of the household sing to her three elaborate songs in a moderate voice, so as not to disturb the hall'!

As in the other countries, the harp was a popular instrument, but as in Scotland it was greatly reduced in popularity because of the hostility of the Nonconformist church ministers. One Welsh writer tells us that

*opposite*
A Welsh harpist wearing the robes of a bard

Because my mother professed religion, and there was a prejudice against everyone who sang with the harp, she would not recite poetry, nor sing in public – but she would, for all that, hum songs during her work at home in Dolgelly.

A distinctive form of music for the harp and voice, which is still to be found in Wales, is 'penillion singing'. The harpist plays a tune. The singer selects a traditional lyric. He must then improvise a second tune over the harp part, using the words he has chosen. Naturally it must harmonise, and fit with the rhythm of the harp music, and it must also finish exactly at the same point.

Dancing was also popular in Wales, though under pressure from the church ministers it died out. Apparently Welsh women were tough creatures, for one writer says that there were dancing competitions, and that 'It has frequently been the case that a merry Welsh lass has danced three men down to the great amusement of the company!'

## The decline of folk music

Folk music began to be less popular when people moved to the cities, and especially after the building of the railways in the first half of the nineteenth century. However, it did not die out at once, for it still had many important purposes to serve.

In the north of England people used folk music to help them protest against the dreadful working conditions which many had to suffer. For example, the weavers suffered terrible unemployment and poverty as a result of the introduction of new machinery, and sang:

We held on for six weeks, thought each day were
    the last;
We've tarried and shifted till now we're quite fast;

We lived upon nettles when nettles were good,
And Waterloo porridge were t' best of us food.

In view of such conditions, it is no wonder that people were driven to violence, even though the punishments were harsh:

Come all ye croppers stout and bold,
Let your faith grow stronger still,
For the cropper lads in the County of York
Have broke the shears at Fosters' mill.

The wind it blew, the sparks they flew,
Which alarmed the town full soon,
And out of bed poor people did creep,
And run by the light of the moon.

## Street musicians

If a folksinger moved to the town, he could become a street musician. This was harder than one would think because, though there were no motorcars, there were many other forms of music competing for the public's attention, and these were often louder and more modern in style than folk music. Perhaps commonest were the organ grinders, who would walk through the streets pushing a mechanical organ or piano, often with a performing monkey to catch the attention of passers-by.

Often the poor old street singer had to compete not only with one other person, but with a whole band. Small brass bands, often from Germany, would set up at a suitable point in the street and play hits of the day, and especially the German waltzes which were becoming all the rage (see pp. 129–31). Sometimes they would travel around the countryside as well, thus bringing a new taste in music to the younger country people, and so helping to speed along the decline of the older folk music.

An organ grinder with his monkey – something still spoken of, rarely seen

## Ballad singers

The street singer's main chance of an income was to work for a ballad publisher. The singer would go around the streets and to public events selling copies ('broadsides') of the words of new ballads. It was calculated in 1861 that there were at least seven hundred such singers in London alone.

A typical employer, and the most famous one, was Jeremy Catnach of Newcastle, who moved to London in 1813. He set up a business in Monmouth Street, Seven Dials, an area near the Charing Cross Road. He paid the ballad writer a shilling, and it is interesting to note that this fee was for the words of the ballad. Often the writer did not have a tune; in

A German band performing in the street in 1879

this case they were sung to any traditional tune that would fit. It is also important to realise that Catnach was not a musician – he kept a resident fiddler on the premises to enable him to hear what was proposed. In this way he was an early and very successful example of the change which took place in the nature of popular music in the nineteenth century. Instead of being a folk activity, with music made by people for those who lived around them, popular music became a business, in which musicians were employed to make profits for businessmen who often knew little or nothing about music. This point will be taken up in the next chapter.

The ballad seller would issue ballads about any topic that seemed likely to sell, but increasingly the best sale was for violent and gory murder ballads. For instance, public interest in the Maria Marten murder case, in 1828, was so great that a million copies of ballads on the subject were sold.

This type of ballad was particularly popular among the crowds who flocked to public executions, which were continued until 1865. At first the ballads acted as newspapers, telling the story of the dreadful crime, but increasingly the 'last confession of the murderer' (made up by the ballad writers) won the biggest sales. A part of 'The Confession of James Macdonald' runs:

This girl she was a servant girl, and I was a farmer's man.
All in the County of Oxford we went walking on the green.
And when she told me what ailed her, I gave her this reply:
'O Annie, we will go no further, for here you have to die'.

'O James, think of your baby dear, and do not give me fright.
Don't think of double murder on this dark and grisly night.
I pray to God all on my bended knee, that if you'll spare my life,
I'll promise never more to trouble you or ask to be your wife'.

But what she said was all in vain, I swore I'd hear no more,
And I cut her throat with my clasp knife, and left her in the gore.
And when I seen her body a-lying on the ground,
I turned and quickly run from there, where I should not be found.

Catnach made a lot of money out of such ballads,

and spent it all. His singers only scraped a living, though, unlike the weavers of Lancashire, they did not have to live on nettles. But really their time was running out. The development of mass circulation newspapers meant that the news could be passed on faster, more accurately, and in more detail. By 1871 there were only four ballad presses left – there had been seventy-five in 1800. Many singers gave up. But the more enterprising moved into the pubs and beer halls, first selling their songs from table to table, and then performing in front of the patrons. Those who were able to win over this audience became the first music hall artists.

**Folk music collectors**
An important difference between classical music and folk music is that folk music is not normally written down – it is passed on by ear. As a consequence, when folk music began to decline in popularity, much of it was soon forgotten completely. So in 1855, members of the Society of Antiquaries of Newcastle had to report, after trying to collect folksong in Northumbria, that they had 'come half a century too late'.

Fortunately there had always been a few people who were interested in finding and writing down the old songs. In the seventeenth century Samuel Pepys, the famous diarist, had collected some 1,800 ballads. Another important collection of that period was that of Thomas Durfey. In the next century much important work was done by Bishop Percy and Joseph Ritson. Many old ballads would have been lost for ever if the worthy bishop had not had the good fortune to enter the room where a maid was about to light a fire with a unique old manuscript. It is believed that she had already burned the only letters of

Shakespeare which had been known to exist!

In the nineteenth century particularly important work was done by two clergymen, the Reverend John Broadwood, and the Reverend Sabine Baring-Gould.

At first the activities of such men were seen as peculiar by their friends. For example, Lucy Broadwood described the difficulties of her father, when he was collecting in Sussex in the years around 1843, as follows:

> He was before his time in sympathising with the dialect, music and customs of country folk. Family tradition describes the polite boredom with which his traditional songs, sung exactly as the smocked labourers sang, were received by his friends and relations. His accuracy of mind, excellent ear, and real love for old things combined to make him a valuable pioneer. When Mr Dusart, the Worthing organist, was asked to harmonize Mr Broadwood's collection, he made great outcries over intervals which shocked his musical standards. A flat seventh never *was*, and never *could* be! And so forth. To which it is recorded that Mr Broadwood, confirming his intervals by frequent blasts on his flute, replied '*Musically*, it may be wrong, but I *will* have it exactly as my singers sang it.'

The greatest name in English folksong collection is that of Cecil Sharp, after whom the headquarters of the English folk music movement, Cecil Sharp House in London, is named. He collected widely in England, and later (1916) in the southern Appalachian mountains of the United States. There he was assisted by Maud Karpeles, whose book on English folk music remains perhaps the finest introduction to the subject.

In 1898 Sharp founded the Folk Song Society. A sign of the changing attitude to folksong at that time was the fact that several of the leading classical composers of the day were founder members – among them were Stainer, Stanford, Parry and Elgar.

Sharp was also the first man to stress the value of traditional folk dancing. On Boxing Day, 1899, at Headington, near Oxford, he saw morris dancing (see pp. 120–3) for the first time. This inspired him to found another society, to learn and preserve ancient dances. In 1911 the two joined forces to become the English Folk Dance and Song Society. As a result of the efforts of such enthusiasts, school and college teachers became interested in the old dances; it is for this reason that most children learn some of them in school to this day.

**Recent trends**
Since about 1950, and especially in the 1960s, interest in folk music has greatly increased, especially among young people. There have, however, been some important changes of attitude to the music since the time of Cecil Sharp.

Originally, folksong collectors and folk singers wished to preserve the older music exactly as they had found it; if they made new songs of their own, these had to be strictly in the old style. This was and is the attitude of artists such as Ewan MacColl and A. L. Lloyd. They felt that it was important to hold firmly to this position, since they believed that commercialism had changed and affected the nature of popular music very much for the worse.

Recently, another attitude towards folk music has emerged. Groups such as Steeleye Span and Fairport Convention felt that folk music was just an earlier form of popular music (see pp. ix–x), and that

Dave Swarbrick, a traditional folk musician, finds a new form of expression through the amplified instruments of rock

popular music has always been quick to use any new material that takes its fancy. They therefore sought to take in and use the new influences of rock and blues when making their music. This attitude is the one taken in this book, and in the series. But you should not forget that many people violently disagree, arguing that commercialism was and still is fatal to the older folk music; as you will see later, there is much truth in what they say.

Whichever of these arguments is correct, we can certainly be grateful to all those who have dedicated themselves to the collection of our traditional music. Without their sustained and enthusiastic work, we should be much the poorer, both in our knowledge of good music to sing, and of the lives and history of our ancestors.

# 2 Looking forward
## folk music in the United States

It may seem strange that there should be a chapter on American folk music in a book which claims to be devoted to the subject of music in Britain. However, there are good reasons for this. First, much American folk music came originally from Britain. Second, to know something of what happened to British folk music in America over the centuries will help you to understand how American popular music, even the most modern, came to be like it is.

**Emigration from Europe**  Between about 1600 and 1900 many people from all over Europe emigrated to America to settle in the vast new lands which had been discovered there. They went for a variety of reasons. Perhaps the most common was to escape persecution (which was the reason that the group of Puritans known as the Pilgrim Fathers went there in 1620). Another important motive was to escape poverty (which was the reason that large numbers of Irishmen went there in the 1840s, during the terrible potato famine of that period).

People from Britain settled on the east coast of America, since that was the nearest point to Europe; the north-eastern area of the USA is still called New England. Different nationalities tended to settle in different areas. Thus so many Scots settled in Nova Scotia (Canada) that Scots Gaelic is still widely spoken there. But people also mixed a great deal and it is this mixing which has made the USA what it is today.

The settlers took with them the songs, ballads and dances which they knew in England. Songs that were too purely English dropped out of use, but many survived and are still sung today. Examples are 'Barbara Allen' and 'The Frog's Courtship'. Because so many people went to escape religious persecution, religious songs were very important – they account for half the older folksongs of the USA. Indeed, religion is still very important to Americans, so much so that there are radio stations, especially in the south, which broadcast only religious programmes.

Since so much depended on contact with Europe by sea, and since for a long time a boat was the quickest way to travel from north to south, we find that sea shanties are a very important part of American folk music. Thus some of the most memorable shanties, such as 'Shenandoah', are American in origin.

The settlers also took with them their knowledge of traditional dances, but again some changes came about. Traditional ceremonial dances, such as the morris, sword and maypole dances (see pp. 120–3) died out. What remained were the country dances, that is, dances in sets by pairs. These dances were simplified in some ways, and became the American square dance, which is still very popular in the USA. The dance was led by a caller, and the music was played on a fiddle. Its Scottish and Irish origins can still be clearly heard in the music.

The first settlements were in the north-east of the

USA, and the music there became what is now known to collectors as 'Yankee folk music'; it retains great similarities to traditional English and Celtic folk music. However, quite soon after, the south was also settled. But being a long way – many hundreds of miles – from the north, it is not surprising that a somewhat different style developed; this is known to collectors as 'the southern folksong'. Finally, as men started to push west in the nineteenth century, the third major group of American folksongs, the 'cowboy songs', were created. These mixed features of both northern and southern songs. They have a very strong Scottish and Irish influence in their use of the pentatonic scale.

Traditional music is still to be heard in the USA, but it has suffered a great deal from the coming of industry, and of many more immigrants of different nationalities from the original settlers. American folk music was also affected by the process which will be described in the next chapter – the influence of classical music, resulting in a new urban popular music.

**Music in the south**   In the south things changed more slowly, since the people were mostly country dwellers, and lived in small, remote communities. British folk music gradually became influenced by hymn tunes (southerners tend to be intensely religious), and by the music of the many black slaves who were brought from Africa to work on the cotton and tobacco plantations. The result was 'country music', which, in the period after the First World War, became commercialised and amplified 'country and western' music. This music still has touches which have come through from Elizabethan times, both in the language of the lyrics, and in the harmonies of the backing. As is well known, country music became an important influence on rock 'n' roll, and later still on singers such as Bob Dylan. These developments are explained in *Rock 'n' Roll* by Dave Rogers and in *Contemporary Folk Music* by Brian Carroll.

There has been one aspect of American history which has affected the development, not only of American popular music, but that of the whole world. This was the fact that black slaves were imported from Africa. Their music was totally different from that of Europe, especially in the fact that it was largely based on drumming, and so was highly rhythmic. As Graham Vulliamy's book shows, the slaves mixed their own ideas with ideas from the European music they heard – in the first instance this was church music. From this mixture came the 'spiritual' and the minstrel show (see pp. 73–9). Later came blues and jazz, and, out of them, all modern pop. At first black people made their music for themselves; nobody knew, or wanted to know, about the music of slaves. But it later became obvious that this music was very exciting, and it was listened to by more and more white people.

However, white folk music was not ignored. In the 1930s some Americans felt that easier transport and the radio could destroy their heritage of folk music. So men such as Charles Seeger went out to collect and record all the folk music they could find. This led to an enormous interest in the music, especially by young people who found the music of Tin Pan Alley too sweet and sentimental. Again as Brian Carroll shows, this interest led to the music of Bob Dylan and all who followed him.

# 3 Times of change
## music in the towns before 1800

**New work, new tastes**

### The effects of industry and town life

In order to understand what happened to popular music after about 1700, we need to think a little about how life changed in that period. Clearly, when conditions change (for example if people earn more money) their life changes as well.

From the time of Queen Elizabeth I onwards, Britain became increasingly involved with foreign trade. The amount of goods to be traded grew very rapidly, once man had invented machines to work for him. At first the machines were worked by wind or water power, but in 1769 James Watt invented his steam engine. After this, men soon discovered how to make the new type of engine drive machines, such as the looms which weave cloth. Unlike a man, a machine never gets tired. Also it can be made to do more, faster than a man – consider how many men would have to work very hard to move the amount which can be carried by one lorry.

It was soon realised that an owner can have more than one machine – he can group them together in a factory. Once this happens, there are several results. Towns spring up and people want their houses to be as near to the factory as possible. There is therefore very little land left for growing food – the towns become heavily built-up. The people who work in the

The machine takes over: one of the last street musicians (in 1925). Ready-made songs, thanks to the phonograph

factory are kept busy making goods – clothing, for example. But if they are doing this, they cannot be ploughing the fields. They come to need *service industries*, such as bakers and greengrocers. Workers are needed to transport food from the countryside, as well as to bring the raw materials which the factory needs. So, instead of one man doing all that is needed to support his family, the work is done by many people. This we call the division of labour, and, as we shall see, this process became as important to music as to any other area of life.

### Professionalism in music

When so many goods are being made, great possibilities for making money arise. The successful then have money to spend, and time to fill – they begin to look for entertainment, for which they are able to pay. It thus becomes possible for people to live by meeting this need – professional artists are required. And where there are professionals, more music is created, and standards rise very rapidly, since there is no need for the musician to stop playing in order to weed the garden or milk the cow.

There had always been some professional musicians, who lived by their skill and, out of pride in that skill, had decided to unite into 'companies' of musicians. These were in practice rather like a modern trade union. Their task was to keep up standards by means of examinations and apprenticeships, and to protect the jobs of their members by preventing non-members from obtaining work. The first of these companies began in 1469, when Edward IV gave a charter to the Fraternity of Minstrels of England, giving them the power to 'examine the pretensions of all who exercised the minstrel's profession, to regulate, govern and punish'.

Another source of employment had been to become one of the town waits. These musicians formed a band which had to provide music for all civic occasions. In return they received a salary, a uniform, and an expensive silver chain as a badge of office. The City Corporation also purchased any new instruments. The number of musicians involved was fairly small; London, for example, had nine.

Originally the waits were watchmen who kept guard over the city at night, and also patrolled the streets, calling out the time. Later they became full-time musicians, and, since the posts were much sought after, the standard soon rose. In the time of Queen Elizabeth I it was written of the Norwich waits that

> few cities in our realm have the like, none better; who besides their excellency in wind instruments, their rare cunning in the viol and violin, their voices be admirable, every one of them able to serve in any cathedral church in Christendom for choristers.

It was also possible to live as a musician without being a member of an official group such as the ones just described. Such performers were known as 'travelling minstrels'. But they were not popular with the authorities. Professional musicians disliked their competition, and the leaders of society saw them as immoral. Laws were therefore made to control minstrels. A law of Henry VIII lists a typical punishment. The minstrel who enters a market town shall be 'tied to the end of a cart naked and be beaten with whips through the same market town until his body be bloody by reason of such whipping.'

If there had always been professionals, how can one claim that the coming of industry changed things? The answer is that the variety and amount of work changed. This can be shown from the account, given by the eighteenth-century historian, Dr Burney, of the violinist John Ravenscroft. Here was a man with a talent which, in earlier times and with his social background, would have made him a folk musician. Instead, he became one of the waits of Tower Hamlets, London, and from there developed such skill as to be able to play everywhere music was needed – he must have been not unlike the session musicians of today. Dr Burney wrote:

> John Ravenscroft was one of the waits of the

Tower Hamlets and in the band of Goodman's Fields playhouse was a ripieno violin, notwithstanding which he was a performer good enough to lead any such concerts as those above described, and to say the truth, was able to do justice to a concerto of Corelli or an overture of Handel. He was much sought after to play at balls and dancing parties, and was singularly excellent in the playing of hornpipes, in which he had a manner that none could imitate.

Briefly, then, Ravenscroft played in the theatre, at concerts, and for dancing; and it was the first two of these which were new areas of employment for musicians.

**Music in the theatre**
The first professional theatre in Britain was built in London, by Richard Burbage, in 1576. Others followed, of which the most famous was Shakespeare's Globe Theatre. These theatres were built on the South Bank of the Thames, outside the control of the City of London authorities. Later, in 1611, the first indoor theatre, the Blackfriars Playhouse, was built, though it was only open to the upper classes and not to the general public.

The nature of the Elizabethan theatre is now well known. It had an apron stage, and no scenery. Boys played all female parts. Acting took place in the open air; there was no artificial lighting. The audiences stood. They soon become bored, and if an actor did not speak up, or the play was dull, there would be a lot of noise, missiles were thrown, and fighting would break out. The City authorities were always complaining about the theatres as places which stirred up the apprentices to fight; the situation was very similar to that at modern football matches.

It is therefore clear that though music was an important part of many plays (Shakespeare's plays are full of music) the musicians had a hard task. The music was provided by small bands, some of whom were actors, while others played in taverns and such places for extra cash. One group, Sneak's Noise, was so popular that Shakespeare mentions it by name in his play *1 King Henry IV*. They played a range of music. As well as trumpet calls, death marches and atmospheric music, there were special compositions, notably for the lute. Songs were very popular. Every good comedy had to have its songs, and these were particularly well received when sung by boys. It was also a tradition that plays should end with a jig performed by the company comedian. By all accounts this was rather like 'Knees Up Mother Brown'. Some critics felt that a jig was an unsuitable ending when the play was a tragedy, but it made no difference. The audience loved it, especially as the dance was often full of indecent gestures.

We still have some of the music from plays of the period. All Shakespeare's lyrics are available, of course, and have often been set to music by later composers with great success.

Such was the position until the Civil War. Then, in 1642, the theatres were closed, the Puritans taking a long-awaited opportunity to put down such dens of sin. The theatres remained closed until the Restoration of King Charles II in 1660.

At an early date after the reopening, theatre managers, influenced by the growing popularity of Italian opera, realised that plays could use a great deal of music. This was a most important outlet for all musicians, since there was a need for singers, composers, performers, and a director or conductor.

At that time, there was also a great need for new material. Since the possible audience was quite small by today's standards, a play could not be repeated many times (it could not have a long 'run'); thus a steady supply of new compositions was needed.

It is work mentioning that the atmosphere of the theatre was very different from what it is today. Nowadays, the theatre is seen as art; people feel that they should be respectful and attentive to what the playwright has to say. But in the seventeenth century things were different; our forefathers expected to be entertained, and if they weren't they soon let the artists know. So Addison, writing in the *Spectator* newspaper of 1711, says of an opera:

> The chorus in which that opera abounds gives the parterre frequent opportunities of joining in consort with the stage. This inclination of the audience to sing along with the actors so prevails with them, that I have sometimes known a performer on the stage do no more in a celebrated song than the clerk of a parish church, who serves only to raise the Psalm, and is afterwards drowned in the music of the congregation.

At least this involved attention to the play. For many the playhouse was no more than a meeting place, somewhere to go to be seen, and to eye women. Sir John Etherege, in his play *She Wou'd if She Could*, describes how the young gallants go

> From one playhouse to the other playhouse,
> And if they like neither the play nor the women,
> They seldom stay any longer than the combing
> Of their periwigs, or a whisper or two with a friend.

Other accounts show that conversation was by no

means always in a whisper!

When an artist was not liked, audience behaviour could be more aggressive. One account tells that 'Ann Barwick, who was lately my servant, had committed rudeness last night at the playhouse by throwing of oranges and hissing when Mrs L'Épine, the Italian gentlewoman, sung.'

## Concerts and critics

Concerts, like the theatre, were not a totally new idea. For example, in 1552 the Norwich City Council noted:

> This day it is agreed by this House that the waits of this city shall have liberty and licence every Sunday at night and other holidays at night, betwixt this and Michaelmas next coming, to come to the Guildhall; and upon the nether leads of the same Hall next to the Council House, shall betwixt the hours of six and eight of the clock at night, blow and play upon their instruments the space of half an hour, to the rejoicing and comfort of the hearers thereof.

But the rapidly changing way of life in the cities meant that it was possible for people to make more money from their work. When they had the money, they wanted to use it to enjoy their leisure time, and one way of doing this was to go to concerts. Many people wanted music frequently, and at a lower price than the cost of keeping three or more minstrels, which was the way in which the very rich provided themselves with music.

In 1672 John Banister, the leader of the King's Own Band, had the idea that there was such a demand. So he placed the following advertisement in the *London Gazette* of 30 December 1672:

> These are to give notice that at Mr John Banister's
> house (now called the Music School) over against
> the George Tavern in Whitefriars, near the back of
> the Temple, this Monday will be music performed
> by excellent masters, beginning at precisely four of
> the clock in the afternoon, and every afternoon for
> the future, precisely at the same hour.

A contemporary music lover, Roger North, described
the scene:

> Banister's room was rounded with seats and small
> tables, alehouse fashion. One shilling was the
> price and call as you please . . . There was very
> good music, for Banister found means to procure
> the best bands in town.

The audience consisted mainly of shopkeepers and
workmen.

The idea of a concert was so obviously a good
one, that Thomas Britton, a coal dealer of
Clerkenwell, London, who was therefore known as
'the musical small coal man', used a loft over his
storehouse at Jerusalem Passage to put on weekly
concerts. The room was narrow and uncomfortable,
but the music was outstanding, and it soon became
a regular event for genuine music lovers, even those
among the aristocracy. The composer Handel was
the most famous of the many fine performers of the
time who played there. The concerts began in 1678
and continued until Britton's death in 1714.

With the rapid expansion of music, the average
music lover needed advice as to what events were to
take place. Also, as he did not have time to keep up
with new musical developments, he needed
guidance. As a result there was another division of
musical labour. Some people became music critics
for the new magazines and newspapers; this is an

employment which is still important today, for the same reasons.

**Taste and social class**

We have already noted that music differed according to area, and between town and country; it was also stated that music differed between the social classes. Why was this?

The factories permitted people to make money, and so did the towns which sprang up around them. In the villages people did not need a greengrocer, for instance, since people grew their own food. In a town, people had to be supplied with food in great quantities. If you only make one penny profit from each customer, but you have ten thousand customers, you soon become well-off. So it was that a certain number of people, factory owners and shopkeepers especially, became much richer than the ordinary working people. Being proud of their achievements, such business people sought to distinguish themselves from the ordinary workers who had not been as successful. Also they liked to use their money to make the quality of their lives better. Between the worker and the nobleman there arose a new middle class, who wanted their own type of entertainment, including their own type of music. As we shall see later, this fact accounted for much of the variety of popular music which existed in the eighteenth and nineteenth centuries.

**Classical music takes over**   The new music which the middle class took up was a form of what we now call 'classical music'. Gradually the popularity of this type of music spread, until even the most popular music was based on the classical style. Popular music was largely created and performed by classically trained musicians. This meant that folk music fell even more out of favour. But what *is* classical music?

### The growth of classical music

To answer this question we need to go back in time, and right away from Britain, to Italy in the sixteenth century. There, as you will find from books about the history of classical music, composers became interested in writing music which was based on Italian folk music. This music was different in styles from the folk music of Britain. Partly the newly composed classical music was paid for by the rich. But it was also paid for by the general public; for example, in Italy opera was liked by ordinary people, who paid to go to opera houses.

The ideas of Italian composers began very rapidly to affect the thinking of composers in other countries, and especially in France and England. The music which was liked by the King of France was in the new style; it was based on Italian and French popular music and was light on the ear and people could dance to it. When King Charles II fled to France to escape from Oliver Cromwell and the Puritans in 1649, he heard the new music, and returned to England full of enthusiasm for it.

Another factor helped the spread of classical music. As we have already seen, folk music was passed on by ear, from person to person. This, together with the fact that communications were difficult, meant that new ideas spread very slowly, if at all. But the new classical music could be taught by being written down (whereas few folk musicians could write down words, let alone music). In 1503 an Italian, Ottaviano Petrucci, showed that music could be printed. After that, people who lived far from each other could obtain and learn the new music.

**Differences between classical and popular music**
If you were a man from Mars, several things would strike you about the differences between classical and popular music. Classical music is made by professional musicians for an audience which does not dance or sing along. Generally, the music is not designed for a particular purpose or occasion in life, such as a wedding or funeral. To hear classical music, we go to special music centres (concert halls) and we sit quietly and listen. Much of the music heard is instrumental, though we can go to a special music centre (the opera house) to hear singing, and to see dancing (ballet). This dancing and singing is not like the dancing in which we take part at a disco, or the singing of someone who is washing up. It is specially composed, and sung or danced in styles which are very difficult to perform and require years of training. We watch professionals perform for us, in the same way as we watch clowns or trapeze artists at the circus.

When the music is sung, there are further differences to note. Our pop songs and folksongs tell us about meeting a girl, doing our daily work, going to a rock 'n' roll dance. The songs of classical music are often about remote times; they may refer, in ways difficult to understand, to things with which we are unfamiliar. Many are based on some form of religious belief. Furthermore, much of what is sung is not even in our native language – it may be in a foreign language, such as German, or even a dead language, such as Latin. Modern concert music is even more different from everyday popular music, since it often appears to have no identifiable tune or beat. To many listeners, it just seems as if men in waiters' costumes appear, look solemn, read music, and make strange and often unpleasant sounds. The

*opposiite*
Classical music
became strongly
associated with
upper-class
audiences and
concert
performances.
(Contrast with
frontispiece)

audience goes away puzzled and doesn't come back.

All this shows why classical music is not like pop and folk, and that it is not interested in being so. It is interested in a world of the imagination, and in new ideas and musical techniques. And because it is made by professionals who have nothing else to do but look for ideas and improve their techniques, while we, the audience, do something else for a living, the distance between the musician and the audience soon becomes very great. The musician is following a line of thought at a much faster rate than the audience because he has time to specialise. The same thing has happened in the sciences.

Popular music is different. It is *functional*; that is to say, it is designed for a purpose, even if that purpose is only to be an accompaniment to washing the pots – which is an important purpose to those who have the boring job of doing it every day. The popular music audience will not buy the music if it does not get across straight away. It must therefore use catchy tunes and rhythms; you must be able to understand it at once, without special training.

**Musical snobbery**
Because the new music was made by professionals who sought out new ideas, it was full of interest and excitement. Before long, popular music came to seem simple-minded, unlike the new music which seemed more complex and subtle. Being less easy to listen to, it was felt to be 'serious' rather than 'light'.

Furthermore, the music had a great deal of status, since it was popular with the upper classes. Popular music was the music of the lower social classes, who used music for dancing and communal singing, not

for concert listening. Thus classical music came to be seen as a 'high class' music. Those who liked it were felt to be superior, both in class and mental quality. For example, in 1899 Sir Hubert Parry wrote:

> The modern popular song reminds one of the outer circumference of our terribly overgrown towns . . . It is for people who live in those unhealthy regions, people who have the most false ideals, who are always scrambling for subsistence, who think that the commonest rowdyism is the highest expression of human emotion; for them this popular music is made, and it is made, with a commercial object, of snippets of slang.

Such an attitude can only be described as 'snobbish'. The writer clearly has little real understanding of why people who live in poor and difficult conditions act and respond as they do. Worse, he has not the grace to admit his own good fortune in being one of the small minority who can escape the tediousness of work and the pressures of money.

You might think that such attitudes vanished with the horse and carriage, but you would be wrong. For example, in 1957 a pamphlet concerned with musical education in schools had the following to say:

> The musical ideals of jazz are in general of a low order. It thrives on distorted tonal values; both the instruments and voices are encouraged to make sounds which are not just different from what we are used to, but definitely less beautiful, less pure and noble. It appeals mostly to the less civilised part of one's nature – the purely physical, the more violent emotions.

Whatever would the writer have said about Jimi Hendrix or punk rock!

Popular music lovers have had a hard time trying to get experts, critics and teachers to realise that to think this way is to go up a blind alley. Pop music is a different sort of music, for a different purpose. It has many good qualities, and there is no doubt that some of its artists are better than others. But they are not trying to do the same thing as the classical composer, and if we believe that they are, we shall never understand or enjoy either of them properly. A car and a motorcycle are both means of transport, but what their owners want from them additionally is very different. If you want to be dry in a storm, don't ride a motorbike!

At first the conflict between the two areas of music was not too marked. But it is noticeable that Dr Burney continued his remarks about John Ravenscroft as follows:

> It seems that this was a kind of music which of all others he most affected; so that by dint of a fancy accommodated to these little essays, he was enabled to compose airs of this kind equal to those of the ablest masters; and yet so little was he acquainted with the rules of composition that for suiting them with basses he was indebted to others.

This comment (which could be applied to most popular artists today) shows that it surprised Dr Burney that Ravenscroft could play dance music too, or that a dance musician could be good at the classics. Even more surprising to him was the fact that Ravenscroft *preferred* hornpipes.

By the middle of the nineteenth century, the popular musician was under constant attack, and the gulf between composer and audience was becoming wider. In the 1880s the composer Sir Arthur Sullivan could still write popular comic operas, but he disliked having to do so, and saw it as an inferior type of work. In the twentieth century the gap became impossible to bridge. The musical language of popular music was left far behind by 'serious' composers, and was criticised as being hopelessly old-fashioned. Fortunately this did not bother popular artists overmuch!

# 4 Music and the middle classes

## Music and social class

It is easy for us, in an age of social welfare and widespread opportunity, to forget that, much less than a hundred years ago, England was a country in which divisions between the social classes were very marked. At one time, people were restricted to their social positions by law – we have already come across the laws about becoming a bard in early Wales, and the ones concerning travelling minstrels in Tudor times. By 1700 many of these laws had disappeared, but people were nevertheless restricted to the class into which they had been born, partly by a lack of money, and partly by social snobbery. For example, to progress in many fields one needs education; but this costs money. Someone must pay. Nowadays this is made possible by the government, but at one time you had to find the money yourself, which needed education, for which you needed money – and so on.

Social divisions were also made very clear by people's attitudes; the books and newspapers of the period reflect this all the time. For example, in Anthony Trollope's book *Dr Thorne*, published in 1858, a major character is Roger Scatcherd, a stonemason. Trollope (who in the book is critical of snobbery) tells us that 'A short time before the days of Henry Thorne's death he [Scatcherd] had married a young wife in his own class of life.' Later Scatcherd becomes rich and is given a knighthood.

Dr Thorne nevertheless tells his niece that Scatcherd 'is good in his way; but they are neither of them in your way: they are extremely vulgar.' At another point the writer tells us that:

> Lady Scatcherd was no fit associate for the wives of English baronets; was no doubt by education and manners much better fitted to sit in their servants' halls; but not on that account was she a bad wife or a bad woman.

It is clear that hard work, skill, money or virtue did not make up for the disadvantage of being born into the wrong social class.

As a consequence of this situation it is largely true to say that entertainment was class-based, that is, that it was designed for a particular class of people. The middle class could afford more expensive entertainment, which in turn provided more opportunities for musicians. On the other hand, those who paid the bill naturally only wanted entertainment which fitted in with their own attitudes towards life.

**Concerts**

One form of middle-class entertainment which grew very rapidly was the concert. It was for this market that the great composers wrote. Large numbers of people went to concerts, and very many performers could be involved. The symphony orchestra may use between fifty and a hundred players, which, compared to a pop group, is an enormous number; but this was only a start – one work by Mahler uses a thousand performers. Big concert halls, such as the Albert Hall in London, were constructed,

Vauxhall
Pleasure
Gardens in the
late eighteenth
century

containing hundreds and even thousands of seats. In
the open air even more people could be catered for.
The open-air concert is not a new idea; in the USA in
1872 the waltz composer Johann Strauss played to
over 100,000 people.

### Pleasure gardens

The open air was also the setting for much lighter
entertainment. In London several pleasure gardens
opened. The most famous were those at Marylebone
(1688), Vauxhall (1732), Ranelagh (1742), and the
Cremorne Gardens (1831). These places sold meals,
put on firework displays, balloon ascents and other
spectacles. Dancing was an important part of the
activities. Above all, the gardens were an important
meeting place, especially for young people, since in
a city one can be very cut off from others. However,
as they became more and more popular, the
standard of behaviour got lower, and rowdyism

increased. For this reason the last of the gardens, the Cremorne, was closed in 1877.

**Theatres**

An important form of middle-class entertainment was the theatre, which grew very rapidly in popularity after about 1700.

After the Restoration, theatres were designed with the now familiar 'picture stage', and scenery became an important element in productions. At one time, for instance, the Sadler's Wells Theatre had a water tank under the stage to add to the production of the nautical dramas which were then popular. At first, as in the days of Shakespeare, rich gentlemen were permitted to sit on the stage itself; this was discontinued after 1763.

It is important to realise that at first there were very few theatres, and that, even though theatres did exist in the provinces, most were in London. A superb example of an eighteenth-century theatre which can still be seen is in Bury St Edmunds, Suffolk.

In 1737 the government became very worried about the tendency of playwrights to criticise them. They therefore brought in a law to say that all plays must be submitted to the Lord Chamberlain for censorship; this law was still in force until a few years ago.

**Musical drama**

In the time of King Charles II, a monopoly for producing *spoken* drama was given to two London theatres – Covent Garden and Drury Lane. 'Straight' stage plays could not be performed elsewhere. However, the demand for entertainment was not to be stifled, and there was no law against *musical* performances, so those who wished to start theatres got round the law by putting on plays which contained a great deal of music. In fact the law helped to reinforce what was already a growing taste.

One form of musical entertainment was the opera, which was imported from Italy. But these lengthy and sober tales of Ancient Greek heroes were a heavy diet indeed after the big dinners which were the taste of the time. There was therefore a market for something less demanding; in this way the comic opera developed, the history of which can be found in other books.

Another form of light musical drama was the ballad opera, the first famous example of which was *The Beggar's Opera* (1728). This had the advantage of having an easy and sentimental story, in English, and of being full of good tunes, which, being simple and traditional, were certain successes!

In the nineteenth century the demand for light opera continued, especially as serious opera became even more serious and lengthy under the influence of German composers. The work of Offenbach, notably *Orpheus in the Underworld*, was a great success here, as well as in its native France. And later still the Gilbert and Sullivan operas, such as *The Mikado* and *The Pirates of Penzance*, which were put on at the Savoy Theatre, London, were incredibly successful, as they remain to this day.

In the 1890s another form of musical theatre appeared; this was the musical comedy. It could be literally comic, that is, with jokes and so on, or it could be just a very romantic story set in an exotic place. The first big success of this type was *The Geisha*, which was set in Japan. Such scripts gave the producer a chance to use lavish scenery, and this, combined with pretty girls and attractive tunes –

Marie Studholme
in *The Geisha*

many of which are still well known today – meant that many of the shows were a success on a scale which had not been seen before. Possibly the most popular of all the musical comedies was *The Merry Widow*, written by an Austrian, Franz Lehar. Another very popular musical comedy, which is still regularly performed by amateur operatic societies, was *Merrie England*, by Edward German. When you see a performance it shows how much attitudes have changed in this century, since it is full of very patriotic songs.

## Pantomime

In 1702 John Rich put on at the theatre at Lincoln's Inn Fields, London, a performance which is now seen as the first pantomime. At first pantomimes were based on the Italian story of Harlequin and Columbine – only later did nursery tales become the basis of the script.

Probably the most famous artist in pantomime was Joseph Grimaldi (1781–1828). He started young, first appearing on stage at the age of two! As he grew older he became noted as a clown, and it is because of this that clowns are still often known as 'Joey'. His greatest success came from 1806 onwards, when he appeared at Covent Garden in *Harlequin and Mother Goose, or The Golden Egg*. In this he sang, danced and did acrobatics, as well as a comedy routine. The latter was 'slapstick' comedy – he would use a coal scuttle as a helmet, for example. He had a particularly famous hit number in 'Hot Codlins'. This was a song about a roast-apple seller who drank too much:

A little old woman her living she got
By selling hot codlins, hot, hot, hot!

Joseph Grimaldi
on stage

And this little old woman who codlins sold,
Though her codlins were hot, she felt herself cold;
So to keep herself warm, she thought it no sin,
To fetch for herself a quartern of——

And here the song would break off without Grimaldi pronouncing the dreadful word 'gin', with uproar from the audience while he sang a chorus of nonsense syllables such as 'Ri tol di li do'. Thus humour changes in 150 years.

Sadly Grimaldi did not heed his own advice, and died of alcoholism while still only in his forties.

### 'Family entertainments'

Though theatres were popular, they were by no means so with everyone. Many people saw them as far from respectable both in the matter of the shows they put on and in the audiences they attracted. The other main entertainment of the period, the music hall (see pp. 89–111) was regarded with even greater distaste by the respectable. For example, the London newspaper the *Standard* claimed in 1878 that 'The open air dissipation of the Cremorne Gardens has been replaced by the indoor dissipation of the halls.'

The respectable middle class therefore looked for another form of entertainment, and especially one to which they could take their often large families. The most important of these was the minstrel show (see pp. 73–9). But also popular with some were the 'illustrative gatherings' run by Mr and Mrs German Reed 'to provide dramatic entertainment for that class of society which was reluctant to visit theatres.' This class was numerous enough to enable the 'gatherings' to continue from 1855 to 1895. Among the centres which put on performances suitable for families were St James', Piccadilly, and the Agricultural Hall, Islington. The latter was ideal for the many members of the growing lower-middle class (meaning clerks and other semi-skilled or partly educated people), who lived in the new suburbs such as Holloway and Islington. It was among these people, who were very aware of their new status above that of the uneducated and unskilled workers, that respectability was most valued.

When such people went on holiday, they liked a similar form of entertainment. This was provided both indoors in halls and small theatres, and also outdoors, in the form of the pierrot show. The first of these was the Clifford Essex Pierrot Banjo Team, which appeared in July 1891 at Henley Regatta. Songs, comic acts and instrumental solos were performed by a versatile but sometimes rather unskilled team of entertainers. The shows could take place under cover, on the pier, or on the sands (weather permitting). English weather being what it is, they rarely made much money, but they survived, and the experience gave a valuable grounding to many who later became well-known popular entertainers. Such shows, or something like them, can still sometimes be seen at the seaside.

As we have seen above, in the nineteenth century there was a large amount of ready-made theatrical entertainment being offered to the middle class. The descendants of these forms are still to be found in the 'politer' seaside resorts, and in many London West End theatres. However, we shall leave them now, because at the very moment when Mr and Mrs German Reed were retiring, and the pierrots were getting under way, a new medium appeared which was totally to revolutionise dramatic entertainment – the film.

## Drawing-room music

We found above that many middle-class fathers did not approve of theatres, music halls and so on, since they saw them as centres of immorality and vice, and extremely unsuitable for their womenfolk to go to.

A pierrot group with its mobile theatre (note the piano), Wimbledon, September 1913

Yet their wives and daughters did not go to work since it would not have been seen as 'proper' for them to do so. These ladies therefore had time, money and the inclination to be entertained in an age without radio, television or record players. They turned, naturally enough, to home-made entertainments such as reading (including reading aloud), gossip, dinner parties, party games such as charades, and, of course, music.

At the centre of the musical activity was usually a piano – for most families an upright, but for richer people a grand. The instrument had first been used in public in England by Charles Dibdin at Covent Garden in 1767, when it was billed as 'a new instrument called piano-forte'. Its range of possibilities and dynamics (loud and soft) made it rapidly popular. It was an excellent means of accompanying songs and of entertaining oneself.

Music making in the drawing room: a Victorian lady plays the harp whilst her children dutifully sing

Unlike the guitar (in its earlier stages), the piano was demanding enough to keep young ladies out of mischief, and it was an instrument at which it was possible to be extremely graceful. It showed off perfectly the face, neck and arms, the only parts of the body which young ladies of the time were allowed to bare to public view. This made piano playing an appealing activity for the young lady whom decency did not permit to make advances, and yet who wished to find a husband – marriage being the only career open at that time to middle-class ladies.

To some extent the harp shared in this boom. But after a while it fell out of popularity. As one writer put it: 'As the fair performers grew old, the charm of the harp decayed, and although the instrument is still played and taught, it is not cultivated to the extent its merits might seem to warrant.' A reasonable though sad explanation. However, it is more likely that the real reasons were a lack of versatility in the instrument's musical possibilities, and the fact that a harp has to be tuned by the performer (not a professional piano tuner) – a difficult operation.

**The song lyrics**
Since women were so important a part of the market for domestic music, and since marriage was so crucial to the future of young women, it is natural enough that love should have been a major subject for songs. One of the most famous love lyrics, though rather heavy for our modern taste, was the setting by Michael Balfe of Tennyson's poem 'Come into the Garden, Maud':

> Come into the garden, Maud,
> For the black bat, night, has flown.
> Come into the garden, Maud,
> I am here at the gate, alone;
> And the woodbine spices are wafted abroad,
> And the musk of the rose is blown.

Heady stuff!

A very important point to bear in mind is that the middle-class love song always aimed to be beautiful, and also to be totally discreet and respectable. Sexual frankness of the sort to be found in folk lyrics was *never* to be found.

Victorian ladies, and indeed, Victorian gentlemen, liked a good cry; nothing went down better during an evening's entertainment than a really melancholy song. Songs about home were usually of this type, especially after the success of 'Home, Sweet Home' by Sir Henry Bishop (words by an American, John Howard Payne). This song first appeared in a musical play called *Clari, or The Maid of Milan* put on at Covent Garden in 1823. Its success reminds us that many middle-class people *did* go to the theatre, and that the aim of every theatre manager was to include songs which would take the fancy of the audience, and so incline them to buy the sheet music.

Childhood memories were always good for a few tears:

Woodman, spare that tree,
Touch not a single bough;
In youth it shelter'd me,
And I'll protect it now.
'Twas my forefather's hand
That placed it near his cot;
There woodman let it stand,
Thy axe shall harm it not.

When performed publicly, this song is said to have brought at least one elderly man to his feet, to ask with bated breath 'Was the tree then spared?' When the singer Henry Russell answered 'Yes Sir, it was,' there was rapturous and relieved applause!

Even better than a happy child was a dead one:

'Twas in that garden beautiful,
Beside the rose tree bower,
Thy gentle child had guiltless strayed
To pluck for me a flow'r;
I heard, alas!, his feeble scream,
And flew some fear to chide,
His little breast was stain'd with blood –
In these sad arms he died.

Again the music was by Balfe, for a Drury Lane musical of 1835, *The Siege of Rochelle*.

The life of a young lady was really very restricted; naturally enough, she liked a bit of excitement in her music at least. Thus it was that a very popular song was 'The Wolf' by William Shield:

While the wolf on nightly prowl,
Bays the moon with hideous howl,
Gates are barred in vain resistance,
Females shriek, but no assistance –
Silence, or you meet your fate,
Your keys, your jewels, cash and plate.
Locks, bolts and bars soon fly asunder,
Then to rifle, rob and plunder.

Henry Russell (1812–1900) was an enormously popular artist of the time. In addition to 'Woodman, Spare That Tree' (1837), he also made popular 'A Life on the Ocean Wave' (1838), and 'Cheer, Boys, Cheer' (1838). One of his most popular songs was 'The Maniac' (1840). Madness, especially if it sprang from grief, had a great attraction for the Victorians – possibly the most famous example is that of Mrs Rochester in Charlotte Brontë's book *Jane Eyre*. Russell's song went as follows (the ghoulish and demented actions that went with the singing have to be left to the imagination!):

For lo you, while I speak, mark how yon demon's
   eye-balls glare!
He sees me now; with dreadful shriek he whirls,
   he whirls me through the air.
Horror! The reptile strikes his tooth deep in my
   heart, so crush'd and sad!
Aye, laugh ye fiends, laugh, laugh ye fiends!
Yes, by Heav'n, yes, by Heav'n, they've driven me
   mad!
I see her dancing in the hall, I – ha, ha, ha, ha, ha,
   ha, ha!
I see her dancing in the hall.
Oh! release me, Oh! release me –
She heeds me not.
Yes, by Heav'n, yes, by Heav'n, they've driven me
   mad!

The same desire for a mixture of excitement and
tearful melancholy was met by songs such as 'The
Storm' by William Shield:

Now the dreadful thunder roaring,
Peal on peal contending clash.
On our heads fierce rain falls pouring,
In our eyes blue lightnings flash.
One wide water all around us,
All above us one black sky;
Different deaths at once surround us –
Hark! what means that dreadful cry?

The life of the sailor was always good for a song.
For example, 'The Arethusa' (by William Shield) and
'Hearts of Oak' (words by the actor David Garrick,
music by the composer William Boyce) were regular
favourites, and indeed are still sung today. The most
prolific writer of sea songs was Charles Dibdin
(1745–1814). He was commissioned by the naval

authorities to write sea songs of a strongly patriotic nature at the time of the Napoleonic Wars, around 1800. He did so with such great success that he was awarded a pension. Typical of his work were these lines from 'Poor Jack':

Why, I heard our good chaplain palaver one day,
About souls, Heaven, mercy, and such;
And my timbers! What lingo he'd coil and belay,
Why, 'twas just all as one as High Dutch.
For he said how a sparrow can't founder, d'ye see,
Without orders that come below;
And many fine things that prov'd clearly to me,
That Providence takes us in tow:
For, says he, do you mind me, let storms e'er so
  oft
Take the topsails of sailors aback,
There's a sweet little cherub that sits up aloft,
To keep watch for the life of poor Jack.

It is worth contrasting this lyric with the genuine songs of sailors, the sea shanties. The latter tell a very different tale, as do the records of the time, which show that conditions at sea were appalling, and that protest against them was a breach of discipline, which was enforced with punishments of anything up to one thousand lashes.

To give the above writers their due, Dibdin's most famous song, 'Tom Bowling', was inspired by the death of his brother, a naval captain, and William Shield had been a boatbuilder's apprentice.

Though they liked to be entertained, the Victorians also liked their songs to be sober and uplifting to the spirit; they expected a good moral, clearly stated. It was an age of cheap liquor, no licensing laws in the way we think of them today, and widespread drunkenness. A very popular theme was therefore temperance, that is, the giving up of all alcohol.

> Father, dear father, come home with me now,
> The clock in the steeple strikes three.
> The house is so lonely, the night is so long,
> For poor weeping Mother and me.
> Yes, we are alone for Benny is dead,
> And gone to the angels of light,
> And these were the very last words that he said:
> 'I want to kiss Papa good night'.
> Come home, come home, oh father, dear father,
>     come home.

The song-copy cover shows a little girl pleading with the stopout, drunkard father.

Closely linked with this tendency to preach morality was a great interest in religion. As we shall see later, Victorian religion was often very sentimental and emotional by modern standards. But the popularity of religious pieces such as 'The Holy City' well into the present century was quite amazing. It is still frequently requested on Radio 4. Another religious song, Sir Arthur Sullivan's 'The Lost Chord', sold half a million copies.

But the middle classes were not always long-faced; they also liked to laugh and to play what we would now consider rather childish games. Among the most humorous of their lyric writers was Thomas Hood (1799–1845). He was, like all Victorians, very fond of puns:

> Ben Battle was a soldier bold,
> And us'd to War's alarms;
> But a cannon ball took off his legs,
> So he laid down his arms.
> Now as they bore him off the field,

Said he, 'Let others shoot,
For here I leave my second leg,
And my Forty-Second Foot'.

**The minstrel shows**    Minstrel shows were mentioned on page 63, in the section on family entertainments, but they were only mentioned in passing. This was because they are so important to our theme that they need a section in themselves.

As soon as Europeans began to travel, they discovered a very different way of life in Africa. It is hard for us to imagine today how strange the two races, African and European, seemed to each other at that time. At a very early point the rich began to import black people to act as servants and to be a curiosity, a kind of strange souvenir of far-off and exotic places. Much less to the white man's credit, he quickly came to see in black Africans a source of free slave labour – workers who don't need be given any wages, and just enough of the necessities of life to permit them to work. An account of this period is given in Graham Vulliamy's *Jazz and Blues*.

It was soon noted that the music of black people was different. Indeed, it must have been amazingly so to our ancestors, in view of the fact that the music with which they were familiar was mostly like that of Mozart or Beethoven. Public interest was soon aroused when imitations of black songs, together with accompaniments on the banjo (an instrument used by the black American slaves) appeared around 1790. One of the most popular of these songs was 'The Gay Negro Boy', composed and sung by Gottlieb Graupner in the opera *Oroonoko*. Though American in origin, this song became popular in England too.

Thomas Rice performing 'Jump Jim Crow'. Under the humour lies a feeling which is grotesque and disturbing

But the beginning of the real boom in interest in music of Afro-American origin came in 1836, when the American entertainer Thomas D. Rice was looking for new material. He saw an old black man in the street, singing a little song, and doing a strange dance consisting of a hop, a skip and a jump. The chorus went as follows:

Wheel about an' turn about an' do jis' so,
An' ebry time I wheel about I jump Jim Crow.

Rice added a comedy routine, which, like so much comedy of earlier times, doesn't strike us as very funny. For example, at one point he fell down, and then sang:

Dis head, you know, am pretty t'ick,
'Cause dere it make a hole,
On de macadmis road,
Much bigger dan a bowl.

(Hilarious laughter and demands for an encore from the audience!)
Obvious Rice did not think especially highly of black people. Indeed, the term 'Jim Crow' passed into the language to describe the attitudes of the type of white people who regard black people in a patronising or contemptuous manner. But though since the American Civil War there have, of course, been white people who disliked or even hated the black man, it is not true to believe that Rice felt that way. Rice's real failure, from our modern point of view, was that he (and people like him) did not even realise that they had any duties at all towards the feelings of people so different from himself as black slaves and servants. We can also be certain that Rice was equally quick to make fun of lower-class white people (compare the attitudes expressed by

Anthony Trollope, see pp. 55–6); the nineteenth-century comedian felt free to make fun of *anyone* who was different, even if it was a difference in appearance caused by a disfigurement of some sort.

Sometimes also the balance was restored by events. For instance, in order to appear, Rice used the clothes of a black stevedore named Cuff, who had to stand shivering in the wings. As the encores went on and on, Mr Cuff tried to attract Rice's attention. He hissed, whistled and called out to no effect. Finally, losing his patience, he walked onto the stage demanding his clothes – the curtain was quickly lowered!

Nevertheless, Rice had broken through to be a big success, both in America and abroad. He was widely imitated. This led soon to the idea of a minstrel show, in which a group of white artists, made up 'in blackface' (that is, coloured with greasepaint or burnt cork) copied aspects of black people's customs and behaviour. There would be singing, dancing and jokes, with a chairman known as Mr Interlocutor. There was a special form of parade dance called the Cakewalk. The most famous minstrel companies were those of Edwin P. Christy, and the Moore and Burgess Troupe (run by George Washington Moore and Frederick Burgess). Though American, these companies became internationally known, and were popular even in the highest circles – at one time the Prince of Wales (later King Edward VII) took banjo lessons.

*opposite*
The minstrel as a family entertainer. Another stereotype – the black man as a simple friendly soul

At first the appeal of the shows was in their distinctive Afro-American quality, but as time went on it was clear that the market could be even greater, and more permanent, if some typically European material was included. Very soon, the shows came to feature a large proportion of drawing-room songs.

It was because of this taste that the songs of Stephen Foster (1826–64) became so popular. Despite the fact that many of his most attractive and successful songs are about the deep south of America, and about black people (for example, 'Poor Old Joe' and 'The Camptown Races'), Foster, a white American composer, appears never to have been there, and indeed to have had relatively little contact with black people at all. His songs are much more European in basic mood than Afro-American, and in fact when his songs were first performed by the Christy Minstrels, he did not want to associate with 'minstrel' material at all (success seems to have changed his opinion!):

> As I once intimated to you, I had the intention of omitting my name on my Ethiopian songs, owing to the prejudice against them by some, which might injure my reputation as a writer of another style of music, but I find that by my efforts I have done a great deal to build up a taste for the Ethiopian songs among refined people by making the words suitable to their taste, instead of the trashy and really offensive words which belong to songs of that order.

The taste for minstrel songs continued throughout the century. Thus Flora Thompson tells us in her book *Lark Rise to Candleford* that in one Oxfordshire village the Squire would appear annually with his minstrel troupe, in blackface, dressed in red and blue, and rattling bones. By this means, the Squire was able, among other things, to express his disapproval of the new ideas about evolution in the work of the scientist Charles Darwin:

> A friend of Darwin's came to me –

'A million years ago' said he,
'You had a tail and no great toe.'
I answered him 'That may be so,
But I've one now, I'll let you know –
G-r-r-r-rr-out!'

Flora Thompson tells us that this was 'emphasised by a kick on Tom Binns' backside by Squire's boot'. (What would Stephen Foster have thought?)

Meanwhile in the music halls which had sprung up around Britain (see pp. 89–111), some of the greatest and most popular entertainers were appearing in blackface. Most notable were G. H. Eliot ('The Chocolate Coloured Coon', 1882–1962), whose most popular number was 'I Used to Sigh for the Silv'ry Moon'; Eugene Stratton (1861–1918), originally a performer with the Moore and Burgess troupe, and made famous by his songs 'Lily of Laguna' and 'Little Dolly Daydream') and G. H. Chirgwin (1855–1922). This last artist illustrates the amazing changes in taste which can come about in only a few decades. He was known as 'The One-Eyed Kaffir', because he left a white diamond of unblacked face around one eye. He sang in a thin voice, yodelled, and played a one-stringed fiddle. His great number was 'My Fiddle is My Sweetheart' – now totally forgotten. And yet he is said to have been second only to the great Marie Lloyd (see pp. 107–11) in popularity.

As everyone will know, interest in the minstrel show has never entirely died out. *The Black and White Minstrel Show* was always one of the most popular of television shows.

Linked with the popularity of minstrel shows there was an increasing interest in black artists and in genuine black music. Early in the nineteenth century

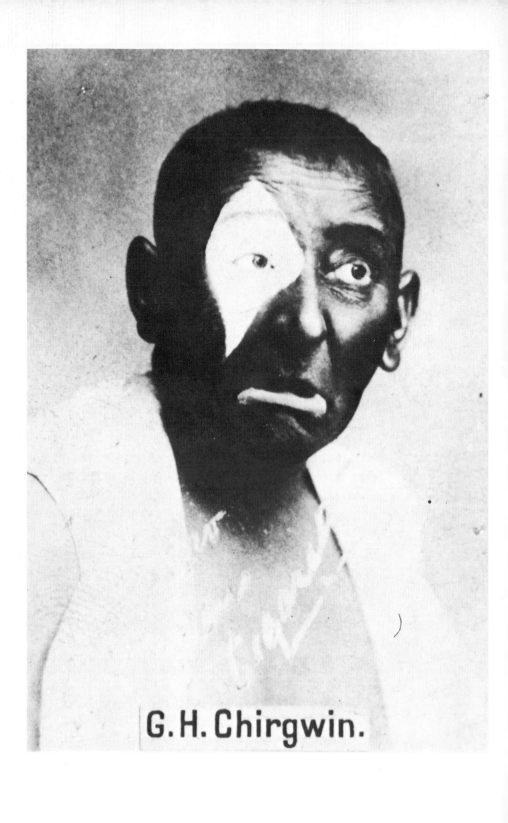

G.H. Chirgwin.

The Fisk University Jubilee Singers who played a major part in making popular the *real* music of black Americans

G. H. Chirgwin – 'The One-Eyed Kaffir'. Perhaps the strangest example of the minstrel fashion

the actress Fanny Kemble, travelling in the southern states of America, had been struck by the 'strange and wild songs' of the black boatmen. These were probably a form of shanty with a strong blues influence.

As the century passed, black artists began to make a name for themselves. Among the most famous was James Bland (1854–1911), composer of 'Carry Me Back to Old Virginny' (his first big hit), and 'Oh Dem Golden Slippers'. In England a sensational reception had been given, in 1848, to Juba, an outstandingly talented black dancer, and later, in 1871, to the Fisk University Jubilee Singers. It was they who made popular 'Deep River', 'Swing Low, Sweet Chariot', and 'Nobody Knows the Trouble I've Seen'. It was through them that the genuine 'spiritual' became known and loved by white people.

But this was not all. The tumultuous receptions they had (ten thousand people at an open-air concert in Hull, for instance) was in part due to the powerful rhythmic effect of their music; it must have had what jazz lovers later came to call 'swing'. The gripping excitement of authentic black music had begun to be felt, and within twenty years, ragtime, the first internationally popular Afro-American musical style, was sweeping the world.

# 5 Religious music
## a music for all classes

The importance of religion to our ancestors has been mentioned before, notably on pages 6–8. It is worth saying again that *all* classes of people attended church. The music described below was therefore the music best known to most people, and the music most loved and respected by them.

**The development of religion in Britain**

Before considering the music, it would be useful to make clear some of the main stages in the history of religion in Britain. These were:

1 The whole of Britain was Catholic until the Reformation, which was begun by Henry VIII in 1536.
2 The new form of religion was called Protestant. In England there were two main branches of Protestant belief – the Church of England, and, later, the Nonconformists. The Nonconformists were stricter in attitude, and did not have bishops.
3 Ireland remained Catholic. Scotland and Wales became mainly Nonconformist, and the Scottish and Welsh churches were very opposed to popular music (for examples, see pages 20–4).

**The music of different churches**

### The Church of England
The Church had always attached great importance to psalm singing; after the Reformation the

congregation expected to join in. The parish clerk would sing a line, which would be followed by the congregation. Apart from psalms there were anthems, which were religious songs with fairly complicated music, sung by the choir. In time it became clear that people wanted good, simple tunes with religious words, to join in with: these were the first hymns. Hymns really started to become popular in the eighteenth century. However, it was not until 1860 that the church produced what is still one of the main collections of hymns – *Hymns Ancient and Modern*. It has sold millions of copies all over the world.

An important point to remember about hymns is that they were not only performed in church. For many people they were a regular, important and popular part of music making in the home. Hymns also helped to fix in people's minds an idea of 'good music'. For example, hymns tend to be very 'square cut', having four lines (an even number, which balances) of equal length. Such music remains popular to this day, and most popular music of before about 1965 had a similar 'square', balanced shape. The harmonies of hymn tunes, which were heard played on the organ, or sung by the choir, also helped people to become familiar with the way in which classical music was written. Quite quickly other types of music, such as folk music, came to be seen as peculiar or wrong. You will remember the problems which Mr Broadwood had, when he wished to write down music which did not conform to the classical and hymn-tune style (see page 30).

Another aspect of the popularity of church music was that ordinary people wished to sing in the choir (this had not been permitted before the Reformation). They were even prepared to pay to do so, and, having learned to sing, they often became jealous of their skill and were very cool towards newcomers. One example was the experience of Thomas Holcroft, a stable boy of Newmarket, Suffolk. One day in 1757 he heard pleasant sounds coming from the church. He went inside and asked the choir master, a Mr Langham, a breeches maker, if it was possible to join. Holcroft later wrote that the choir said

> they should be very glad to have me, for they much wanted a treble voice, and all they required was that I should conform to the rules of the society. I enquired what those rules were, and was told, they each paid five shillings entrance, five shillings a quarter to Mr Langham, another five shillings for *Arnold's Psalmody*; and they paid forfeits of pennies and twopences, if they were absent on certain days, at certain hours, or infringed other necessary bye-laws.

Another way in which people took an active part in religious music was to join one of the church bands, which usually played in the gallery. In 1642, an order had been made by the Puritans that churches should not have organs, and most of those that were in existence were destroyed. Since an organ is a very expensive instrument, it was not until about 1800 that it again became common in the smaller country churches. So, in the same spirit as Mr Langham's choir, the local inhabitants would often form themselves into a band, for the purpose of accompanying the services. In the nineteenth century the bands died out, their job being taken over by the organ.

Religious music was also very popular when performed outside the church service; interest in such music was the major reason for the rapid and widespread growth of choral singing (see pp. 117–19). Above all, people wanted to sing oratorios, that is, long works on religious themes. The first of these to become popular was Handel's *Messiah*. To do this some learned to read music, and some to read sol-fa (see pp. 117–18). In this connection, a striking demonstration of the interests of young people at that time is shown by the fact that in October 1843 John Curwen, the founder of the sol-fa movement, announced that he would give a singing class on Monday and Tuesday evenings 'to which those children would be admitted who were fond of music'. Just after 8 p.m. no less than seventy young people were waiting for a lesson. And Curwen noted that 'an earlier hour could not be chosen, as many of the children do not leave work till eight.'

### The Nonconformist churches

An important factor in the success of the Methodist Church was that they encouraged congregational singing, at a time when many Church of England clergymen were opposed to it. The founder of the movement, John Wesley, wrote 'Directions for Congregational Singing', as well as making a collection entitled *Sacred Melody*. In the Preface to the latter work he wrote: 'Learn these tunes; sing them exactly as printed; sing all of them; sing lustily; sing modestly; sing in time; above all, sing spiritually, with an eye to God in every word.'

'Sing lustily' is an instruction which tells us much about the success of the Methodists (which was very great in the eighteenth and nineteenth centuries). The Church of England had become a very moderate church, whereas in the Methodist movement the emphasis was on an extremely emotional form of worship. Wesley's sermons moved people very greatly (literally to tears) and the hymns had the same effect.

At various times after the success of Wesley, there were similar highly popular movements, which offered an easily understood and emotional type of religion; these are known as 'revivalist movements', because they revived religion to a more lively and popular form. Probably the most famous of these movements was that of two now forgotten Americans – Dwight L. Moody and Ira D. Sankey. Sankey composed many simple tunes, which now seem very old-fashioned and sentimental to us. Probably the most well known nowadays is 'There were Ninety and Nine', which can still be found in the *English Hymnal* (number 584). At the time both the hymns and the message they carried were tremendously popular – Moody and Sankey claimed to have 'reduced the population of Hell by a million souls'.

The success of the Jubilee Singers (see pp. 81–2) was also partly due to this spirit of revival in late-nineteenth-century England. In 1873 they appeared at Mr Spurgeon's Tabernacle in Hull. They sang 'to a crowd that filled the street farther than the voice of either speaker or singer could be heard. Tears trickled down the cheeks of many to whom the sound of prayer or religious song was apparently almost unknown.'

Finally, we must mention the success, at about the same time, of the Salvation Army (founded in 1878). At first their intentions were mistaken. Because they wore uniforms they were thought to be an unpatriotic military organisation, and they were set upon by angry and suspicious hooligans. But they did not give up, and were quick to use music to appeal to the public. For instance they took the tune of

Religious revival. This picture illustrates the enormous popularity of Moody and Sankey

'Champagne Charlie' (see p. 93) and turned it into a hymn.

The late nineteenth century was a time when there was a great deal of popular religious music, ranging from Sullivan's 'The Lost Chord', and the big choirs singing *The Messiah* to the Moody and Sankey revival, and the music which was sung by children as part of their daily activities in the new Elementary Schools. This state of affairs changed, along with so many other things, after the First World War.

# 6 Music and the working classes

**The early years of music hall**

When the cities grew, and people moved in from the countryside, they found that their lives had changed in many ways. The old village traditions died out, and the gap that then existed in people's lives had to be filled by some cheap form of entertainment. It was – by the music hall.

The theatres which were described earlier did not provide the type of entertainment which the poorer workers wanted, nor did they charge prices which were within the reach of working men. Consequently there was a large and ready market for the efforts of the street singers who went around public houses. Landlords quickly realised that a small stage in a large back room could be used to present artists as an added attraction to an audience that was going out to drink – as is still true today.

For the better-off, something of this sort had existed since the 1820s, in the form of the 'song and supper rooms'. Among the most famous were the Coal Hole, in the Strand, and the Cyder Cellars, in Maiden Lane. Also in the centre of London was Evans', which was probably the best known of all. Evans' was essentially a man's club, though ladies were allowed in unofficially to watch from behind a grille. The men would eat sausages and mash, and drink stout, while a varied, but to our taste curious, entertainment was put on. This would include songs by choir boys, imitators of farmyard animals, and singers such as Charles Sloman, whose famous piece was 'The Wolf' (some of the words of which are given on page 69).

Credit for starting the music hall as we think of it today (that is, as a lively, working-class entertainment) is generally given to Charles Morton, who in 1848 put on performances at the Canterbury Arms, Lambeth Marshes, London. This move was so successful that in 1851 he built a special hall at the back which seated 1500 people.

The audience was young, under twenty-five as a whole, with a predominance of men – in the earlier days ladies were not normally admitted. This situation began to change in the 1860s, though for a very long time the attitude of the more respectable members of society remained one of great suspicion towards the halls. Food was sold, and originally the audience sat at tables to eat, chat, and, when they felt inclined, to listen to the artists. This layout gave way increasingly to seats, as in the theatres, because you could admit more people and control them more easily.

The performance was organised and supervised by a chairman who introduced the artists (and made extra money when they bribed him to make comments in their favour). A good chairman was usually seen as 'a bit of a character'. The behaviour of the audience was very different from what would be accepted today. First, the young people had gone there to meet each other, and so were often busy chatting, laughing and moving from group to group. Second, old and young alike became very impatient if an act did not appeal to them. In the earlier halls a net was placed over the musicians to protect them from missiles, and the waiters had their beer bottles chained to their trays to prevent theft by anyone who wanted to drink from them, throw them, or both!

The halls grew very rapidly in popularity, so that according to one estimate there were about five hundred in London by the 1880s. However, there were frequent attacks in the Press upon bad behaviour in the halls. These attacks were supported by the introduction of laws about the management of halls, as the century wore on. The most important of these was the Act of Parliament passed in 1878 which said that halls must have a 'certificate of suitability'. To obtain one of these, the management had to ensure that the stage and the audience were separated, as in a theatre, that there was a safety curtain, and that no liquor was taken into the auditorium. As a result of this Act some two hundred halls were closed, and the nature of the remaining halls changed, as we shall see in the next section.

**Some major artists of the early period**
Many performers attempted to find fame, and more particularly fortune, in the halls. This is not surprising when we realise that earnings could be as much as £100 a week, at a time when most people's income was not much more for the whole year. Success meant escape from poverty and drudgery into a world of glamour and luxury – quite a small sum went a long way in those days. For instance, an ordinary senior office worker could expect to buy a house and employ a maid.

Of the many fine artists of that period, a few are worth a special mention here, namely, George Leybourne, The Great Vance, and Bessie Bellwood.

*George Leybourne* (1842–84) was born Joe Sanders, and was originally a Birmingham factory

CHAMPAGNE CHARLIE

THE GREAT COMIC SONG WRITTEN & SUNG BY
GEORGE LEYBOURNE.

George Leybourne, wearing the dress and striking the posture of a 'dandy', performs 'Champagne Charlie'

worker. He went to work at the Canterbury Arms for 30s. a week. He was so successful that he was given a year's contract as £25 a week. He made his name with 'Villikins and his Dinah', which was a parody of the older folk style. In 1868 he took on the task of publicising a song which was sponsored by the champagne firms in order to advertise and increase the sales of their product. It was called 'Champagne Charlie' and was an instant success; in fact, it was so well received that his income rose to £120 a week. His act was popular largely because of its appeal to the mixture of mockery and admiration which audiences of the time felt towards the type of rich man with a private income, who lived and dressed flashily, and spent his time wandering from one London entertainment to another. Leybourne not only presented this image on stage – he kept it up in his daily life, presenting a dream-like life of wealth, and yet not losing touch with his roots. He wore suits of puce, violet or green, and drove around in a carriage drawn by four white horses. His drink was, of course, champagne, provided by the wine merchants.

Though 'Champagne Charlie' was his biggest hit, he also made popular a song which is better remembered today – 'The Man on the Flying Trapeze'. Like so many music hall artistes, he lived furiously, drank heavily, and died early.

*Alfred Vance* (1839–88), known as 'The Great Vance', was born Alfred Stevens, and was made famous by a range of songs. Among these were songs about the London cockney such as 'Costermonger Joe' and 'Going to the Derby'. But in 1868, the year of Leybourne's success, he performed as Martha Gunn, the bathing-machine attendant. In the middle was a spoken section, which shows us what Victorian humour was like:

> Bathing strengthens the interlect, braces the body,
> puts new life into the blood, old heads on young
> shoulders, fills the pocket, drives away care, cures
> corns, warts and bunions, Pilgrim's Progresses,
> water on the brain, new-ralgia, old-ralgia,
> velocipedes, bicycles, tella-crams, and all the
> Primrose 'ills the flesh is heir to.

Vance was one of the first 'swells'. A 'swell' was a
rich man who dressed very stylishly. Often members
of the upper classes were seen as rather foolish and
empty-headed and were mocked by the music hall
performers. But being a 'swell' was more serious – it
was the image and way of life which you could have
when you were as rich as those who had been your
superiors – the life-style of the man who had 'made
it'. The witty and cynical nature of Vance's act is
shown in his song 'The Husbands' Boat'. Husbands
who were successful in business in London would
come down at the weekend to Margate, when their
wives were on holiday there with the family. This trip
was often seen as a chance to break loose briefly
from the cares both of work and of family life. So,
sang Vance,

> Imagine my surprise, then, I chanced to turn my
>     eyes, when
> i saw a lovely damsel, who was looking straight at
>     me.

> We got in conversation, I stood a cold collation;
> We soon got near to Margate Pier; the time went
>     quickly by.

> Around her taper waist, then, my arms I just had
>     placed, when

I'm Par Excellence, the idol of the day.
London or in France, my time I pass awy.
I'm Par Excellence, in form and field and dance,
In fact in all the sports of life, I am Par Excellence.

The Great Vance
– looking every
inch a 'toff'

I heard a voice that brought me to my senses instantly.

Changing to a high-pitched imitation of a child, Vance would then say:

Oh look, Ma, there's Father. Isn't it kind of him to bring
Your dressmaker with him on board?

This song was another of the big hits of 1868!

*Bessie Bellwood* (1857–96) was one of the first women music hall artists. The fact that she was a woman is important because her career marks the beginning of a change in the position of women in society. Women suffered at least as much as men from the common problems of working people – unemployment and poverty. But until this time there had been even less chance to escape; among other things, it had not been seen as respectable for a woman to go onto the stage.

Bessie was a rabbit skinner from Bermondsey, London, before she made a success in the halls. Her most famous song was 'Wotcher Ria', which tells us a lot about what the cockney felt towards his 'mates':

I'm a gal what's doing very well
In the vegetable line,
And as I've saved a bob or two,
I thought I'd cut a shine.

*opposite*
Bessie Bellwood, here looking sensuous but ladylike – and not at all a person to indulge in slanging matches!

So I goes into a music 'all,
Where I'd often been before;
I didn't go in the gallery,
But on the bottom floor.

I sit me down, quite comfy like,
And calls for a pot of stout;

*opposite*
George Robey

My pals in the gallery spotted me,
And all commenced to shout:

Wotcher Ria!
Ria's on the job.
Wotcher Ria!
Did she speculate a bob?
Now Ria she's a toff,
And she looks immensikoff,
So it's Wotcher, Ria, Ria,
Hi! Hi! Hi!

Though very popular, Bessie was, by middle-class standards, no lady. She had to appear as a replacement for a local star once, and was hissed. One particular member of the audience, a coalheaver by trade, led the trouble. Bessie did not attempt to carry on with her act, but started a slanging match with him, which lasted for nearly six minutes. Then, an account tells us (unfortunately not in detail!):

At the end, she gathered herself together for one supreme effort, and hurled at him an insult so bitter with scorn, so sharp with insight into his career and character, so heavy with prophetic curse, that strong men drew and held their breath, while it passed over them, and women hid their faces and shivered. Then she folded her arms and stood silent, and the house, from floor to ceiling, rose and cheered her until there was no more breath left in its lungs.

## The later days of music hall

You may well have heard music hall songs, though you may not have realised what they were. Most of the songs we know today date from the period between 1878 (the year of the introduction of the certificate of suitability) and 1914 (the beginning

This picture of Kate Carney towards the end of her life is typical of the image of the music hall artist which we tend to have nowadays

of the First World War). During this period there were many successful artists, of whom a few are mentioned below. Unfortunately, space does not permit us to look at other equally important performers such as Kate Carney, George Robey and Vesta Victoria.

## Some major artists

It may come as a great surprise to find that this list begins with the name of *Charlie Chaplin* (1889–1976). We rightly think of him as an outstanding film comedian, but in fact he was born and bred in London, and learned his art on the music hall stage. However, he did not make a name for himself until he went to the USA and began to make films, at the time when the cinema was a very new, but rapidly growing, form of entertainment. He then became probably the most well-known comedian of all time.

Chaplin's way of making films retained many features of the music hall. Like most music hall artists, he had his own characteristic costume – the bowler hat, baggy trousers and stick – and relied greatly on mime, facial expression and slapstick humour. This was vital in the days when films had no soundtrack, before 1927. All his films are funny and worth seeing, but *Limelight* is of especial interest to us because it is set in London before the First World War, and tells the story of a once-great music hall artist at the end of his career. The film gives a good idea of what it was like to be a music hall artist of the time.

*Albert Chevalier* was born in 1861 and died in 1923. Unlike most music hall artists he was middle class in origin, and had first gone into 'legitimate' acting. But he turned to the halls, and with outstanding success. He made his debut at the

Charlie Chaplin.
Compare his
stage costume to
those of
Leybourne,
Vance and
Lauder

London Pavilion, on 2 February 1891, and became instantly popular. His speciality was costermonger songs (a costermonger was a cockney barrow boy); typical were 'The Coster's Serenade', 'The Future Mrs 'Awkins' and 'Down at the Welsh 'Arp'. The latter song was about an August Bank Holiday spent by an artificial lake in Hendon, North London, which became a traditional holiday spot for lower-class Londoners. The sight of the costers in their 'pearly' dress, and driving their small carts, was for a time one of the spectacles of Victorian London.

The songs of Chevalier which we now remember best are 'Knocked 'Em in the Old Kent Road' and 'My Old Dutch'. The latter song is still guaranteed to produce uproarious applause for even the most awful singer, when people have been drinking for long enough at weddings and similar occasions. In Chevalier's act, the curtain opened to show a painted scene of a workhouse (a place which provided the bare essentials of life for the old and unemployed). There were separate entrances for men and women. Chevalier would come onto the stage with his 'Old Dutch'. The workhouse keeper would then indicate that the couple had to go into separate houses. Chevalier would cry out in horror 'You can't do this to us – we've been together for forty years.' Then he would begin to sing:

I've got a pal,
A regular out an' outer,
She's a dear old gal,
I'll tell yer all about her.
It's many years since fust we met,
'Er 'air was then as black as jet;
It's whiter now, but she don't fret,
Not my old gal.

Then the drums would roll, and Chevalier would go into the chorus, with everyone joining in when they weren't sobbing:

We've been together now for forty years,
An' it don't seem a day too much;
There ain't a lady living in the land,
As I'd swop for my dear old Dutch,
No there ain't a lady living in the land,
As I'd swop for my dear old Dutch.

As we have seen previously, the Victorians liked emotion, and they liked it strong – this was true of the drawing room, and it was true of religion, so it is hardly surprising that it should be true of the music hall too. It was this appeal, together with a good moral tinge, which resulted in Chevalier becoming acceptable to the normally superior middle class:

Mrs Ormiston Chant, when the applause which greeted her had ceased, asked those present to think of what they owed to men like Mr Chevalier for making songs like that which had just been sung, that expressed the finest sentiments in the human heart; who had voiced themes that had been there, but before were not voiced, and had done so in a language understood of the people . . . She had sat in a music hall in the poorest part of London where 'My Old Dutch' was being sung, and where the whole audience took up the chorus, and again and again repeated it until one could not listen without the tears coming into one's eyes, and the feeling arising that music like that, taking hold of the public heart might be the means of introducing into lives a tenderness and a sentiment not hitherto displayed.

*opposite*
Albert Chevalier,
dressed as a
costermonger

Though we may now laugh at the emotion of

songs such as 'My Old Dutch', it is worth pointing out that within living memory the possibility of ending one's days in the workhouse was very real; the Poor Laws which permitted this were only abolished when the National Health Service was created in 1948.

The work of *Charles Coborn* was very different. He lived from 1852 to 1945, but his great period was in the 1880s and 1890s. He was famous for two songs in particular. One was 'The Man who Broke the Bank at Monte Carlo' (1891). This was a great success for Coborn, as one might imagine, since the song is still well known today. However, the writer of it, Fred Gilbert, was less lucky. Coborn brought the rights for £10, immediately made £20 from a sale to the publishers, Francis Day & Hunter, and finally made some £600 in royalties. This was not Coborn's first hit, since he had made his name first with 'Two Lovely Black Eyes' (1886), another song which is still sung. This was a parody of the famous Christy Minstrels' song 'My Nelly's Blue Eyes'. The creation of both these songs illustrates very clearly the ruthless nature of the popular music business before the application of the copyright laws (see pp. 112–13).

An artist spoken of with great reverence by those who saw him was *Dan Leno* (1860–1904). He had won the World Clog Dancing Championship in 1878, and then moved into the music halls, where he made a great success. Reports suggest that his great gift was a stage presence, and a talent for mixing humour with sadness which was equal to that of Charlie Chaplin. Unfortunately he did not live long enough to be filmed, so we are unable to judge; one of the essentials of permanent fame is to be born at the right moment. His wisecracks remind one in some ways of Groucho Marx:

I've earned a good deal of butter to my bread –
but I wish it had been spread more evenly.

I love to see the working man, and I love to see
him work.

Work never killed anyone yet, and it shall never
kill me.

You can still see and hear this sort of joke in pub
bars.

### Two famous women
*Florrie Forde* (1876–1940) had a career so
successful that even today almost all the space
available to us must be used just to list her famous
songs: 'Pack Up Your Troubles in Your Old Kitbag',
'Down at the Old Bull and Bush', 'Oh, Oh, Antonio',
'Has Anybody Here Seen Kelly', 'Hold Your Hand
Out, Naughty Boy', and 'She's a Lassie from
Lancashire'. Florrie was Australian by birth, which
illustrates a theme we have met before – the need to
move to find success. Just as country people moved
to the city, and Celtic peoples moved into England,
so people from what was then the Empire moved to
Britain. It is the place which is growing in economic
power which attracts the talented. Thus after the First
World War especially, but even before, as in the
case of Charlie Chaplin, artists emigrated to the USA
in search of fame and fortune – a trend still to be
observed in the careers of rock groups, despite a
brief period of glory for the Beatles and others.

*Marie Lloyd* (1870–1922) was probably the most
popular music hall artist of them all. She was born
Matilda Alice Victoria Wood, and was the daughter of
a waiter at the Grecian Saloon. She came from
Hoxton, East London. Like so many others she saw
the music hall as a way out of poverty. It certainly

worked for her, as after the First World War she was earning £10,000 a year.

She made her debut young, in 1885, at the Falstaff Music Hall in Old Street, with the song 'The Boy I Love is up in the Gallery'. She appeared looking very sweet and innocent in 'a white lace dress, with pink and blue ribbons, and her golden hair right down there, natural . . . and her big blue eyes and her baby's cape of lace. And she came on with a harp and looked like a toy doll.' (The speaker was Marie Kendall, her dresser.) But Marie Lloyd soon learned that she had another side to her talents – a gift for innuendo. This means the ability to put over sexual humour by suggestion, rather than by direct means – for example with a wink, or 'the way she handled her beads . . . and rubbed them across her teeth with that saucy look and that wonderful smile.'

This manner of presentation she added to wonderful songs such as 'My Old Man' ('The Cock Linnet Song' with its line 'You can't trust a Special like an old time copper'), 'Oh Mr Porter' ('What shall I do?'), and 'A Little of What You Fancy Does You Good'. She could also be very witty, putting herself across as 'One of the Ruins that Cromwell Knocked About a Bit'.

However, her gift for innuendo got her into trouble. She was called before the London County Council because her work was giving rise to complaints from the righteous. She wittily defended herself – without the innuendo songs such as 'Oh Mr Porter' are perfectly innocent, and could be sung by children. She then mocked the sober councillors by demonstrating in how lewd a manner Tennyson's 'Come into the Garden, Maud' (see p. 67) could be delivered, if one was so minded. They let her off. However, she was also banned from taking part in

Two images of Marie Lloyd: *opposite* the little girl combining innocence and innuendo; *over page* the blowzy mature woman

the first Royal Command Performance, in 1912. It was felt that the King and Queen would not take kindly to Marie's brand of humour. So she set up another show on the same night and packed the theatre, despite the royal competition!

Both of these incidents illustrate a characteristic of Marie Lloyd which endeared her to the public – she was a great fighter. She was a leading figure in the music hall artists' strike in 1907, for example. She had learned to fight the hard way, by having to win over difficult audiences, much as had Bessie Bellwood. For instance, when she first went to Sheffield, she was 'given the bird' by the audience. She waited patiently until the noise died down, and then said: 'So this is Sheffield; this is where you make your knives and forks. Well, you know what you can do with them, don't you. And your circular saws as well!'

Sadly, Marie's personal life was not so happy. She was unlucky with men, and, like so many of her fellow artists, drank a lot. While still quite a young woman, she collapsed on stage, and died soon after. Her funeral was attended by 100,000 people.

**The growth of a music industry**

During the period 1880–1914, great changes took place in the world of professional music. Before the growth of the cities, as we saw earlier, there had been little professional music (see pp. 38–42). This situation had changed when cities came into being, with rapidly growing populations and new markets. But after about 1880, music ceased to be just a profession; it became a business, with the same characteristics as any other area of industry.

The first big change was after the Act of 1878. This resulted in the closure of theatres and halls which did not have the capital to make the alterations required by the Act. Moreover, various business men, notably Oswald Stoll, recognised that there was an even greater market waiting to be opened up, as the music halls became more widely acceptable. It was clear that much bigger theatres could be built and filled. The layout of the London Pavilion, built in 1885, illustrates what happened. The tables gave way to tip-up seats, and the chairman to a billboard. The audiences rose in number from a few hundred to two or three thousand.

There was also a big market in the provincial cities, and Stoll therefore created a chain of theatres. A good act could then be exploited to the full, being seen in the most places, by the biggest audiences. It became possible to offer exclusive contracts. All this corresponded with the tendency, which had been seen over the past hundred years or so, for businesses to get bigger, and to be able to offer a bigger income to the successful. However, the disadvantage for the artist and the consumer is that at a certain point the market is cornered by a very small number of very big companies – this restricts choice and freedom.

This tendency was aided by the creation and strengthening of the copyright Acts, which assure the creator of a work the exclusive right to make profits from it, unless he or she chooses to sign away these rights. We have already seen in the case of Charles Coborn and Fred Gilbert (p. 106) how little a songwriter could earn, and how his work could be bought for next to nothing, or even stolen. However, in 1886, an international agreement was reached; this was the Berne Convention for the Protection of Literary and Artistic Works. An artist's heirs and publishers were to hold the copyright on his work until fifty years after the publication of the work, or the death of the author, whichever was the later. Until that point no one could use the artist's work without permission and the payment of a royalty. At first not all countries agreed (the Eastern European countries still do not accept this law) and the law was widely ignored.

However, publishers had grown in number and power, and wanted the best return on the money they put in. The growth of publishers is shown by the fact that in 1888 there were one hundred or so in London, and no less than sixty printers of music. The type of sum involved can be illustrated by the fact that a song copy cost three or four shillings – equivalent to a day's pay for an unskilled worker. The 'pirates' who ignored the copyright laws were selling copies at twopence apiece. Clearly the publishers did not wish to allow this to continue. Firms such as Chappells became angry at the fact that others reaped the benefit of the money which the publisher had risked. They therefore tackled the problem by forming the Musical Copyright Association and by employing strongarm men to intimidate the hawkers who 'pirated' work in the streets of London. The law was strengthened in 1902, but it was still not effective enough. The publishers threatened to invest no more money, and Chappells spent a further £10,000 on a prosecution to establish the legal position more clearly. Finally Parliament passed another law in 1906, which meant that anyone convicted could be sentenced to twelve months' hard labour in prison. This resulted in the effective laws which exist today.

The advantage of chains of theatres, big publishing businesses and copyright laws was that the artist could earn more money. The disadvantage was that he was increasingly at the mercy of big business. He

*opposite*
Harry Lauder in
kilt and sporran,
1902

was expected to work very hard, doing several
performances a day, and, unless he was very
successful, being often poorly paid. Conditions
worsened, and finally, in 1907, the artists accepted
that the only way to get any results was in the way
that industrial workers had improved their conditions
– by a strike. This was led by Marie Lloyd and
others. The strike won the support of the public, and
permanent changes were made.

## The decline of the halls

The music hall carried on until well into this century.
Indeed, some of the greatest names date from this
period; for example, there were George Formby
(father of the ukelele-playing film actor), and the
Scotsmen Harry Tate and Harry Lauder.

*Harry Lauder* (1870–1950) revolutionised the
position of the Scottish artist. When he began his
career, it was so uncommercial to present a Scottish
image that he had to pretend to be an Irishman! By
the end of his career, his kilt, bonnet and stick were
world famous – and he could earn £1000 a week.
His successes are very well known today: 'It's Nice
to Get Up in the Morning, but It's Nicer to Stay in
Bed', 'A Wee Deoch and Doris', 'Stop Your Tickling,
Jock', 'Keep Right On to the End of the Road',
'I Love a Lassie' and 'Roamin' in the Gloamin' '.

But artists such as Lauder were the end of a line.
The music hall had to give way to the cinema, which
was new, more spectacular, and cheaper.

## Serious music and the working class

### Social conditions

From what has been said so far, it might seem as
though the working classes were an entirely different
set of people, who never met or mixed with the
middle class, and who had their own music and
interests which never coincided with the tastes of the

middle class. Also the impression may have been gained that among the working class music was merely an accompaniment to nightly drunkenness and revelling.

This was by no means entirely true. There was always some mixing between the two classes, and between the different areas of music. It is true, though, that popular music was increasingly scorned by the educated musician, and also that, if only for lack of money, most working-class people had no chance of getting an education and admission to middle-class careers and pursuits.

Things began to change as more people got the vote, and especially when compulsory education was introduced by the Act of Parliament of 1870. It was necessary, as society became more industrial, to find more trained workers. Such workers needed to be able to read and write, and to have a range of other knowledge. To this pressure was added the fact of a strong religious movement in many areas of the country, especially in the shape of Nonconformism. This belief created a very serious attitude in its followers, helping them to feel that it was right to work hard and advance oneself, and to help others. Such opinions helped to start the Labour Movement. This is the term we use to refer to the situation in which working people began to demand a say in how they were governed (the vote), a better standard of living (employment and wages), social welfare (health schemes and pensions), and more career opportunities (especially through obtaining education). These things may seem common enough to us now, but they were unthinkable a hundred years ago; working men were not thought to have a right to such benefits.

Working people also began to expect more out of

life. The skilled man could hope one day to buy a house, and perhaps even to hire a maid, like the office workers who lived in the suburbs. And as men became more educated, this too inclined them to ask for more in their leisure life. Among other things they became interested in the music which had not hitherto been available to them – classical music.

## Listening and performing

People wanted to hear concerts of classical works. Any such interest was increasingly encouraged by organisations such as the People's Concert Society, which was founded in 1878 to present concerts to the London poor. Music was also held at 'penny readings', at which poetry was also read. It was through such events that the writer Charles Dickens became famous. A concert programme might well include music by sixteenth-century composers, such as Lassus, famous nineteenth-century composers such as Mendelssohn, and contemporary composers who were then popular, but are now largely forgotten, such as Bishop.

However, to listen to music was not enough for some. They wished to sing themselves. But this meant that they had to read music. Classes were started in many cities, but more important in its effect was the invention of the system of tonic sol-fa (that is, the naming of the notes as doh, ray, me, etc.). The system was devised by a Norwich lady, Miss Sarah Ann Glover, but was publicised by John Curwen, who founded the Sol-Fa Association in 1853. From then on, large amounts of music were written out in the system. The method was given a further boost in 1870, when it was included in the training of the teachers who were to operate the new system of compulsory education. Singing was introduced into the school curriculum since it was felt to be good both as an introduction to music, as helping the pupils to know religious music, and as a mental discipline.

Not surprisingly, this led to a steady growth of choirs such as the Hanley Glee and Madrigal Society (1882). There had been important choirs long before this date, however, especially in the north of England. For instance, the Bradford Old Choral Society started in 1821, and had three hundred singers. The most famous of all, the Huddersfield Choral Society, started in 1836.

Brass band music, too, was already well known to working people. There were military bands which could be heard regularly, and also the small travelling German bands, whose repertoire was quite 'highbrow' at times. But now working men had the desire to form bands of their own. One such was at the works of J. & G. Meakin in Hanley, Staffs. James Garner, a noted local musician, persuaded the employers to buy instruments and start a band. This experience is typical of the start of the still thriving tradition of works bands. But the Meakin band was only one of 10,000 on the books of an instrument-making firm of the period. Naturally this led to a growth of concerts, festivals and competitions, the most important of which was the National Brass Band Festival.

Such activities inspired local authorities to put on public concerts. Leeds, for example, began to do so in 1903, at a minimum charge of one shilling and sixpence. In 1909 the cost of entrance had to be put up because the audience had shrunk – to 1300, a figure which would be very good for many modern performances.

In many ways the social classes did live different

A public concert in Battersea Park, London. The brass band was sponsored by the London County Council

lives, and had different tastes. But in the ways mentioned above traditions of music making were started which still exist today. They were the first real and large-scale entry of the working class into the field of serious music.

# 7 Dancing

All the music that has been considered so far was *sung*, either to accompany an activity, or for pure entertainment. It is now time to mention the other main area of popular music – music for dancing.

As far as we know, people have danced since the earliest times – it seems almost instinctive to move to music, as we can see by watching small children. But very little is known about earlier dance music, since it was not written down. Furthermore, until about 1400 there was no known way of writing down descriptions of the steps and movements of a dance – everything was passed on by word of mouth.

It is important to realise that though dancing was a very popular recreation, it was often disapproved of by the church, which was at that time very powerful. The Puritans, especially, saw dancing as closely linked with temptation and sin. So the Puritan Philip Stubbes, demanding that dancing be banned, in 1583, asked: 'For what clipping, what culling, what kissing and bussing, what smooching and slabbering of one another, what filthy groping and unclean handling is not practiced in those dancings?'

**Ceremonial dances**
In the countryside dancing took several forms. The most complicated of these, and probably the most ancient, were various types of ceremonial dance,

most notably the sword dance and the morris dance. These were performed by teams of men who carefully preserved the tradition over hundreds of years.

Morris dances are found in southern and south-east England, and sword dances in the north-east. This division probably reflects the effect of the Viking invasion and occupation of northern England from about AD 700–950. Sword dancers no longer use actual swords, but metal strips known as rappers.

Though there are many differences between morris and sword dances, there are nevertheless many similarities. The most important of these are: a complicated pattern of steps, performed by a team of men, special and unusual costumes, set pieces of music, and performance only on certain occasions, such as Midsummer Eve. This is because the dances were originally part of religious ceremonies to celebrate the passing of the seasons, and to bring good luck to the harvest. Gradually the original point of the dances was lost, but the tradition of performing them continued. However, the serious nature of the festival became changed into an excuse for a riotous holiday. So Richard Baxter, writing in 1696, tells how

One of my father's own tenants was the Town Piper, hired by the year (for many years together), and the place of the dancing was not an hundred yards from our door; and we could not on the Lord's Day either read a chapter, or pray, or sing a psalm, or catechise or instruct a servant but with the noise of the pipe and tabor, and the hootings in the street continually in our ears . . . And sometimes the morris dancers would come into the church in all their linen and scarfs and antique dresses with morris bells jingling at their legs.

The sword dance ends with the combination of the rappers into the *lock*. In this photo of 1900 we see the linking of an old tradition with nineteenth-century taste in costume

The dress, the steps and music, and some of the boisterous spirit are still to be found in morris teams to this day.

Morris dances were learned and practised by special teams. But for most people something simpler was needed. One such dance was that performed around the Maypole. A tree trunk was cut down, set up on the village green, and decorated with green boughs, blossom and streamers. Before the Civil War a morris dance was performed, but it is not certain at what date the villagers began to follow this with a ring dance around the Maypole.

There would also be 'social dancing', that is, dancing for people to get to know each other, and for young people to pair up. The earliest of these social dances was the carole, which consisted originally of both a song and a dance. At first it took

Modern morris dancers try to get back to the original tradition in dress and performance (contrast picture opposite). Notice the bells on the legs – a charm against bewitchment by fairies

the call-and-response form described in connection with the sea shanty, but later the songs were sung separately, and began to use less repetition. It is from these songs that most of our Christmas carols are descended. However, caroles could be sung at any time, and were especially popular in the spring, when people could go outdoors (this was vital, since there were no special dance halls at that time).

When dancing the carole, people joined in a chain, rather as in the modern conga, and danced round in a circle. Circle dances were originally linked with magical ceremonies, but after a time these links were forgotten, and dancing became an opportunity for a very lively good time. It was this kind of behaviour that Philip Stubbes was thinking of.

**Country dances**  In the seventeenth century an important change took place, in that the chain and ring dances which had been popular began to give way to a new style, in which pairs of dancers performed set movements in formations such as lines, squares and circles. These dances were known as contradances (from the Latin 'contra' meaning 'opposite' or 'facing'); the word rapidly became changed to 'country dances'. These became popular throughout society, and remained so in one form or another until the very end of the period covered by this book.

The spread of the new dances was an interesting process. Many dances were originally popular among European peasants, especially in France and Germany. A new dance would be adopted, refined and introduced by the aristocracy at balls. Then the popularity of the dance would spread down the social scale. The most important of these dances were the gavotte, the minuet, the cotillion, the quadrille and the bourrée.

The latter, for example, began as a very boisterous dance from rural France. It could not have been more vigorous, even in the uninhibited twentieth century:

> The couples cross, swing the head and body, raising the arm, snapping the fingers, and noisily hammering out with their feet the beat given by the bagpipes or the hurdygurdy. Rhythm is essential in the Bourrée – to the point where it alone suffices. In the absence of the bagpipe, one may see one of the dancers perched on a table singing the air, while he vigorously pounds out the rhythm with his foot. Finally his humming diminishes, he no longer sings. His heel suffices to keep the couples going until dawn.

This vigorous activity was greatly reduced and refined by the aristocracy, until the dance was finally polite enough to be used as a basis for one of the forms of classical music – a remarkable change.

**Ballrooms** In the eighteenth century the bourrée was not an important dance in Britain, but the minuet, cotillion and quadrille were. These dances were at first performed in private houses, but there were also public ballrooms, notably the assembly rooms in the spas where people went to take the medicinal waters. The most popular were those at Tunbridge, Epsom, Hampstead and Bath (the latter is vividly described by Jane Austen in her book *Northanger Abbey*).

A typical evening was:

6 p.m. Minuets (the dancing being opened by the couple of the highest rank)
8 p.m. Country dances
9 p.m. Rest period and tea served
10 p.m. Country dances

The dance usually finished at 11 p.m. It is noticeable that though the foreign and elegant minuet began the proceedings, the more vigorous local dances took up most of the time. They came in the latter half because they were provided for the younger members of the audience, which contained people of all age groups above the late teens. The young were only given their head after the more high-ranking older people had been given pride of place in the more sedate minuet.

The rules of behaviour at dances were very strict. Young ladies were invariably accompanied by an older female relative. For a girl to have more than a couple of dances with anyone except a near relation

The splendour of an upper-class nineteenth-century ball (given by the officers of the St George's Volunteer Corps at Willis' Rooms, March 1861)

or fiancé was considered very forward, and prejudicial to her marriage prospects. There was also much snobbery. Thus the rules of the Cheltenham Assembly Rooms stated: 'That no clerk, hired or otherwise, in this town or neighbourhood, no person concerned in the retail trade, no theatrical or other public performers by profession be admitted.' Members of these lower classes had to find entertainment elsewhere, at first in the pleasure gardens (see p. 57–8) and later in the specially built halls which were opened in the nineteenth century. The importance of the upper-class dances was that they introduced fashions which the rest of the population later followed. Furthermore they set a standard, which meant that dancing was closely linked to ideas of correct behaviour and respectability.

A great deal of the responsibility for the spread of

new dances, fashions and ideas of good taste lay in the hands of the dancing masters, who were active throughout the kingdom. Those who wished to climb the social scale and to demonstrate their superior refinement would hire a dancing master to teach them elegant dancing, deportment and fencing. There were also travelling masters who hired themselves out to the general public. A description of 1909 from north-east England runs as follows:

> There are still many who remember the visits to our villages of the travelling dancing master. These were men of the working class, and often of a jovial disposition, fond of dancing and good fiddlers. The travelling dancing master would stay in the village for two or three months in winter, and give his lessons in a hired room or a loft lent for the purpose. The members of the class and a few friends paid him a small sum. From time to time he gave a more public dance, which he called a 'small occasion', and at the close of the season a 'grand ball' for his own benefit.

Such masters were concerned with the more traditional dances. But there were many, especially in the towns, whose livelihood was made by teaching the better-off more fashionable modern dances, such as the waltz and the polka. Increasingly dance teachers began to cater for the huge and growing market of lower-class customers. Among the most successful in the late nineteeth century was G. F. Horndale, who ran dances in London at the Arlington Ballroom, Peckham, at the Kings Hall, SE1, and at the Carlton Ballroom, Shepherd's Bush. The price was about a shilling a head, and the Arlington could hold about four hundred people. It is such halls that were the forerunners of the modern ballroom dancing which is still a popular feature on television.

Concerned by their low reputation, dance teachers worked hard to get themselves accepted as professionals. They practised a great deal, invented new steps, ran competitions, laid down rules, and also enforced rules of ballroom etiquette. It is noticeable that even to this day, male ballroom dancers wear tails, and the ladies evening gowns, which are very much the dress of formal upper-class occasions. The similarity to the changes which came over the musical profession should also be noted.

In the nineteenth century, the bulk of the dancing was roughly what we would now call 'Old Time' dancing. A typical programme of 1847 was:

 1 Quadrille
 2 Lancers
 3 Spanish dance
 4 Quadrille
 5 Polka
 6 Caledonians
 7 Cellarius waltz
 8 Quadrille
 9 Redowa waltz
10 Polka
     Interval
11 Sir Roger de Coverley
12 Quadrille
13 Polka
14 Waltz
15 Quadrille
16 Polka
17 Quadrille
18 Circular waltz and posthorn galop
19 Quadrille
20 Polka
21 Quadrille

It should be noticed that the favourite of early Victorian ladies, the polka, was strongly featured – even the young Queen Victoria enjoyed this dance.

**The waltz**    What this programme does not show is the rapid growth in popularity among all classes of the waltz. The importance of the waltz is that it differs from all the social dancing we have mentioned (except the polka, which came after the waltz). People danced in couples, separately (that is, not in lines or sets) and holding each other. The waltz was originally a German peasant dance and is derived among other sources from a dance called the Ländler. But its advantages over the formality of the minuet were soon recognised by the young! Its effect cannot be credited today. Criticism was extremely strong:

> The verb waltzen, whence this weird 'waltz' is derived, implies to roll, wallow, welter, tumble down, or roll in the dirt or mire.
> What analogy there may be between these acceptances and the dance we pretend not to say; but having seen it performed by a select party of foreigners, we could not help reflecting how uneasy an English mother would be to see her daughter so familiarly treated, and still more to witness the obliging manner in which the freedom is returned by the females.

That was written in 1805. Eleven years later things were unchanged, for *The Times* of 16 July 1816 commented on a dance given by the Prince Regent:

> We remarked with pain that the indecent foreign dance called the Waltz was introduced (we believe for the first time) at the English Court on Friday last. This is a circumstance which ought not to be passed over in silence. National morals depend on

national habits; and it is quite sufficient to cast one's eyes on the voluptuous intertwining of the limbs, and close compressure on the bodies, in their dance, to see that it is indeed far removed from the modest reserve which has hitherto been considered distinctive of English females. So long as this obscene display was confined to prostitutes and adulteresses, we did not think it deserving of notice; but now it is attempted to be forced on respectable classes of society by the evil example of their superiors, we feel it a duty to warn every parent against exposing his daughter to so fatal a contagion.

These criticisms had little permanent effect, however, and the waltz was given a further boost by the popularity of the Viennese waltz, largely due to its outstanding composers, the Strauss family. The father had a very exciting stage personality, such that the composer Wagner wrote:

I shall never forget the extraordinary playing of Johann Strauss, who put equal enthusiasm into everything he played, and very often made the audience almost frantic with delight . . . the music was a more powerful drug than alcohol. The very first bars set the whole audience aflame.

Another writer, Heinrich Laube wrote: 'Typically African too is the way he conducts his dances. His fiddlebow dances with his arms, the tempo animates his feet.'

These qualities enabled Strauss to achieve wide acclaim and international popularity. He toured Britain in 1838, impressing the young Queen Victoria, and performing 72 concerts in 120 days, at a rate of £200 per performance. He and his men ended the tour exhausted, for they slept in the coach – it was a life not much different from that of many rock bands today. But the effect of the orchestra was incredible. The *Morning Post* said that 'so perfect a band was never heard before on this side of the Channel.'

The popularity of such music continued throughout the century – the waltzes of Johann the Younger, notably 'The Blue Danube' and 'Tales from the Vienna Woods', are still widely loved. Like his father, Johann the Younger toured, and once played in the USA to an open-air audience of 100,000 people.

The Viennese waltz is a very quick dance, but it is important to note that as the waltz became more popular, its tempo slowed down, and it became more sentimental in nature. This, together with the close hold of the dancers, and the vigour of Johann Strauss, senior, all point to a very important conclusion, which has already been made in connection with the minstrel shows. This is that *popular dancing became more and more appealing to the body*. In 1805 the waltz was 'obscene'; by 1900 the same dance was thoroughly respectable. With every passing year, it became more common for people to throw aside restraints (which had sometimes existed for thousands of years). Perhaps the most striking were those applying to the rights and behaviour of women. More and more, they demanded emotion and excitement from their music. And, naturally enough, this was most true of the young. As John Shepherd's book *Tin Pan Alley* shows, the process of demanding personal freedom, and uninhibited expression has continued into the twentieth century, and indeed continues at this very moment. As this book has constantly tried to show, the seeds of today – *your* time – lie inescapably in the past.

# 8 A last word

The aim of this book has been to tell you something about popular music – the music of the majority of people – before the twentieth century. To end, it is worth summing up, and drawing together a few threads.

1 The earliest form of popular music was folk music. It was closely bound up with country life, and the needs of work, as well as with magic and religion.

2 The coming of industry and the growth of the cities resulted in enormous changes. People left the countryside, and poorer regions, such as Ireland, in order to seek a better life. When they did this their old traditions died out, including the making of folk music.

3 Yet people still wanted entertainment, and they still wanted to meet. So entertainers were needed, and it became profitable for full-time professional entertainers to exist. A new urban popular music was created.

4 Before long, businessmen realised that popular music could be a very profitable field to be involved with. So music publishers emerged, music halls and dance halls were built, and a large and profitable industry evolved. This industry also presented the possibility of great wealth for the successful.

5 Earlier societies were very rigidly divided into social classes, and each class had its own musical tastes. But gradually this situation changed.

6 People with unpleasant or boring jobs demanded exciting entertainment. Increasingly the restrictions of respectability and tradition were broken down. The history of the waltz shows how people were moving towards a music which would appeal strongly to the body.

Earlier music is very different from the music of today, especially if we compare it to heavy rock or soul. But it still has a lot to offer. It can tell us about our roots and ancestry, and can show us how much times change. And it can also show us how in important ways all people have the same dreams and feelings, and have in former times expressed these feelings in tunes still worth singing.

# Glossary of musical terms

**anthem** A religious song based on a biblical text, sung by a choir.

**apron stage** A theatre stage which juts out into the audience.

**ballad** This word has several meanings. In this book it means: (1) a long folksong, telling a story which may be true or fictional. A ballad is often, but not always, in **call-and-response form**. (2) A short popular song (in the phrase **ballad opera**).

**ballad opera** A form of musical drama which became popular in the eighteenth century. It was so called because it consisted of a spoken play containing many **ballads** (that is, short popular songs of the day) rather than specially composed music.

**bard** A professional maker of songs and poetry in the Celtic countries before about 1650.

**bass** The lowest-pitched part in a piece of music. *String bass (double bass)*: A stringed instrument used for playing bass parts. In appearance like a large, upright violin.

**bourrée** (This is a French word, pronounced boo-ray.) A dance popular among French peasants in earlier times, in a lively two-beat time. Expert opinions differ, but it seems likely that it got its name from the French for 'to pummel', or 'beat vigorously'. The dancers pounded the earth with their feet, and possibly struck their hands together as in the **morris dance**.

**broadsheet** A single sheet of paper on which a **ballad** is printed.

**cakewalk** A dance of Afro-American origin which became very popular about 1900. It was performed to **ragtime** and similar music. It resembled a strutting walk, and was originally created in imitation of white employers in the southern United States, during the second half of the nineteenth century.

**call-and-response form**  A method of music making in which a leader (possibly improvising) sings a line (the *call*), and is answered by a chorus (the *response*). The *call* and *response* are usually one-line long each. This procedure is an important part feature of African music, Afro-American music and the sea **shanty**. (For an example see p. 2.)

**carole**  (1) A medieval dance in **call-and-response form**, in which a chain of dancers moved round in a ring. (2) A song in the same musical form as the dance, usually connected with special festivals. Out of such songs came the Christmas carol (note the change of spelling), though Christmas carols no longer follow the original musical form.

**catch**  A piece of music in **counterpoint**, similar to a round. Often the words were indecent. It was sung by gentlemen in the seventeenth and eighteenth centuries.

**ceremonial dance**  A traditional folk dance, with set patterns, performed on special occasions such as May Day and Midsummer Day.

**chord**  The result of sounding three or more different notes together.

**classical music**  A form of music created in Europe, or under a strong European influence, and preserved in musical notation. It is normally intended for attentive listening, either in concerts, or in religious ceremonies. Classical pieces tend to be quite long, and the composer pays special attention to problems of musical form. Though there are many modern composers of 'classical' or 'serious' music, in this book the term refers to music created before 1900. Such music was primarily a middle- and upper-class taste, and was written and performed at its best by professional musicians. *Note*: The term 'Classical music' (with a capital C) is being used correctly only when it is applied to a particular style of the second half of the eighteenth century.

**concertina**  An instrument used by English traditional folk musicians in the nineteenth century. It consisted of a bellows squeezed together and pulled apart, as in the piano accordion, but, unlike the latter, notes were made by pressing a series of buttons, rather than piano keys.

**concerto**  A musical composition which features a solo instrument together with an orchestra.

**congregational singing**  Music sung together by all the people who are attending a church service.

**consort**  The phrase '*in consort with*' means 'together with'.

**cotillion**  A **social dance** of the eighteenth and nineteenth centuries, danced in set figures and patterns, in a lively two-beat time.

**counterpoint**  In a musical composition, the art of combining melodies with each other, or setting them against each other at the same time.

**country and western music**  The music which was most popular with white people in the southern states of the USA after about 1920. (For further details see *Rock 'n' Roll*, pp. 22–9.)

**country dance**  Originally 'contradance'. An English **social dance** performed in sets or lines and face to face, unlike the 'ring dance', popular earlier, which was danced in a circle.

**flat seventh**  (See p. 30.) Much of the music we know today, and also the **classical music** with which Mr Dusart the organist was familiar, is made up out of the major scale. The easiest way to find what this sounds like is to play the white notes of the piano from C to C (see diagram). Mr Dusart was upset because Mr Broadwood insisted that folk singers used a **scale** with a flat seventh. In this case, it would mean that the singer used the black note indicated in the diagram. This note offended Mr Dusart's ear, because it seemed wrong to him, compared with the classical scales which he had studied.

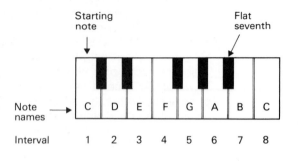

**folk music**  The popular music of one community. In practice, the music of rural societies of the past. Folk music was usually sung, and was passed on by ear. Most commonly it was either *functional* (see pp. 1–4, 4–5 and 50) or connected with special occasions (see pp. 5–8). It was felt to be the property of all, and not just of one person.

**gavotte**  A **social dance** of the eighteenth century, danced in sets and lines. It was in four-beat time, and used a basic rhythmic pattern of

*three four/one* two *three four/one, etc.*

**harmony**  (1) The 'harmony (or harmonies) of a tune' are the **chords** which accompany it. (2) When musicians study harmony, they study the *rules governing the use of chords.* (3) To 'harmonise' a tune is to fit harmonies to it.

**hornpipe**  A dance of the eighteenth century. It was originally danced by sailors, and was a **step dance** in a quick two-beat time, usually performed by one person.

**hurdy gurdy**  A stringed instrument. With one hand the player turns a handle in order to rotate a wheel which rubs against the strings and makes them sound. With the other hand the player makes notes by pressing keys.

**hymn**  A religious song with original (not biblical) words, for singing by a congregation.

**improvisation**  This word has several meanings. In this book it means the act of composing music at the moment of performance, rather than planning it beforehand.

**jig**  A lively dance in a quick six-beat time, found in many countries. In the British Isles it is especially popular in Ireland and Scotland.

**lute**  A pear-shaped instrument, especially popular before about 1700, which is rather like a guitar in both sound and manner of performance.

**lyric**  This word has several meanings. In this book it means *either* (1) the words of a song, or (2) together with the **ballad**, one of the two main types of folksong. The lyric is a short song, sung by one person about one emotion. (For further details see pp. 9–10.)

**metre**  This word has more than one meaning. In this book it means the basic rhythm to which the words of a particular poem or song lyric are fitted. Perhaps the easiest way to pick out a metre is to imagine any limerick you know as a pure rhythm, without the words. This gives *the metre of the limerick.*

**minstrel** This word has several meanings. In this book it means (1) a travelling musician (before about 1600); (2) a professional musician employed by a nobleman (before about 1600); (3) a performer in a **minstrel show**.

**minstrel show** A popular entertainment of the nineteenth century, based on the music, dancing and humour of black Americans. In Britain such shows were performed by white people with black make-up. The same was true in America, but there were also shows performed by black people themselves. (For details see: *Folksong and Music Hall*, pp. 73–9; *Tin Pan Alley*, pp. 18–23; *Jazz and Blues*, pp. 22–3.)

**minuet** A **social dance** of the eighteenth century in slow three-beat time, with very elegant movements.

**morris dance** A **ceremonial dance** popular in the south of England in past centuries. It was danced by a team of men on special occasions, and notably on May Day and at Whitsuntide. A special dress and set steps were used.

**musical comedy** A form of musical drama which became popular in the 1980s. It used specially composed music in a light **classical** style, together with impressive scenery and costumes, pretty girls and romantic plots.

**music hall** A place of entertainment with mostly working-class audiences, popular in Britain between about 1820–1920. The performance would include singers, comedians and other variety artists, such as magicians and jugglers.

**ornamentation** Notes added to a single musical line or melody, to give greater variety or expressiveness.

**parish clerk** The person who led the **congregational singing** of **psalms**.

**parterre** The part of the ground floor of a theatre which is behind the orchestra.

**penillion** A traditional form of Welsh music in which a harpist plays and repeats a set tune. A singer must then choose a suitable traditional lyric, and improvise a second tune to go over the harpist's theme. Both players must finish at exactly the same time.

**pentatonic scale** A set of five notes out of which tunes

are made (unlike the **scale** best known to most people, which is a set of *seven* notes).

**picture stage** The normal stage since the eighteenth century, so called because it appeared to the audience, that they were looking at a framed picture.

**pierrot show** A type of variety show, usually performed at the seaside, after 1891. Whenever possible the shows took place in the open air, for instance on the beach. The performers wore clown costumes, hence the name ('pierrot' is a Continental name for a clown).

**pipe and tabor** A penny whistle and a simple drum, played at the same time by one player. It was a combination which was especially popular at the time of Shakespeare.

**polka** A lively **social dance** in a quick two-beat time, in which the couples hold each other. The dance was originally Polish, but became widely popular throughout Europe in the nineteenth century. Its basic rhythm is: one, two, *three*, rest.

**popular music** Any music which is liked by a very large number of people (a mass audience). Usually, but not always, the musical taste of the majority. Popular music is also often defined, in contrast to **classical music**, as music for which a special training is not needed. This is not strictly correct, but it is true to say that popular music is music which is not normally studied in the music education system (e.g. at music colleges).

**pop music** The music favoured by young people (under 25) since about 1955. The term includes rock 'n' roll, reggae, Tamla Motown, etc.

**psalm** A piece of poetry from the Bible which is chanted in church services.

**quadrille** A **social dance** of the eighteenth and nineteenth centuries. The dance is in four-beat time, and consists of five musical sections. The dancers dance in sets of four couples each.

**ragtime** The first form of Afro-American music to become widely popular with white people (about 1895–1920). It was usually played on the piano, and used a range of characteristic rhythms derived from black American **folk music**. (For further details see: *Jazz and Blues*, pp. 22–4; *Tin Pan Alley*, pp. 26–56.)

**rapper** See **sword dance**.

**reel** A **social dance** in a lively two-beat time, and danced in lines, with circling movements (hence the name). It is especially popular in Scotland, Ireland and North America.

**rince fada** (Irish for 'long dance'.) An Irish **ceremonial dance** of earlier times, danced in long lines, with kerchiefs or ribbons used rather as in the **morris dance**.

**scale** A set of pitches, most commonly arranged in ascending order, out of which musical tunes or compositions are made.

**shanty** A song sung by sailors to assist them while working on sailing ships. It was usually in the **call-and-response form**. The leader who gave the call was known as a shantyman.

**social dance** Any dance whose main purpose is for people to meet and enjoy themselves socially (in contrast to **ceremonial dances**).

**spiritual** (Also previously known as 'Negro spiritual'.) A slow tuneful religious song created by black Americans.

**square dance** A form of **country dance** popular in the eastern areas of the United States. Such dances are derived from British folk dances. The dancers dance in square sets, and are guided by a caller.

**step dance** A dance in which the dancer does not move far, but in which the interest is in complicated footwork.

**strathspey** A lively Scottish **country dance**, invented in the eighteenth century, and named after the area in which it first became popular (Speyside). It was danced in sets, and is similar to a **reel**, but slower.

**suite** A form of classical composition, based on types of dance. Among the most common dances used were the **jig**, the **minuet**, the **gavotte**, and the **bourrée**.

**sword dance** A carefully arranged **ceremonial dance**, from the north of England, performed by a team of men. Instead of real swords, flexible metal bars with handles (called *rappers*) are used. (*Note*: In other countries there are other forms of sword dance.)

**tone** This word has several meanings. Strictly speaking, the word should be used to refer to the quality or character of sound made by *an individual performer*. However, the word is often used instead of *timbre*, which refers to the quality of character of sound made by *a particular instrument*, for example, the timbre (sound) of a violin, as compared to the timbre (sound) of a trumpet.

**urban (popular) music** The music most favoured by the inhabitants of towns and cities.

**viol** An instrument most popular before about 1650, like a violin in appearance, but different in sound and construction.

**waltz** A very popular **social dance** of the nineteenth and twentieth centuries, in which the couples hold each other close, and dance steps in the order they choose (unlike in a **country dance**, where the order is fixed, and the couples do not embrace). Originally it was a fairly quick peasant dance in three-beat time, but it later became much slower. The Viennese waltz is a form of quick waltz developed in Vienna in the nineteenth century.

# Sources and acknowledgments

**Song lyrics**   P. 2, 'The New Times' ('In My Old Mother's Days') from M. Vicinus: *The Industrial Muse* (Croom Helm, 1974); p. 2, 'Blow the Man Down' from A. L. Lloyd: *Folk Song in England* (Lawrence & Wishart, 1967); pp. 2–3, 'The Lavender Seller's Song' from A. R. Warwick: *A Noise of Music* (Queen Anne Press, 1968); p. 6, 'The Cutty Wren' from J. Silverman: *The Folk Song Encyclopaedia* (Chappell, 1975); p. 9, 'Lord Lovell' from J. Silverman, op. cit.; p. 9, 'The Grey Cock' ('I Must Be Going, No Longer Staying') from R. Vaughan Williams and A. L. Lloyd: *The Penguin Book of English Folk Song* (Penguin, 1954); p. 10, 'I Wish, I Wish' from ibid.; p. 15, 'The Gresford Disaster' from E. MacColl: *The Shuttle and the Cage* (Workers' Music Association, 1954); p. 15, 'The Row upon the Stairs' from M. Vicinus, op. cit.; pp. 24–5, 'The Four Loom Weavers' from E. MacColl: *The Singing Island* (Mills Music, 1960); p. 25, 'Come All Ye Croppers' from ibid.; p. 28, 'The Confession of James Macdonald' from C. Sharp: *Folk Songs from Somerset* (Novello, 1904); pp. 61–2, 'Hot Codlins' from J. Ashton: *Modern Street Ballads* (Chatto, 1888); p. 67, 'Come into the Garden, Maud' from *Tennyson: Poems and Plays* (OUP, 1965); p. 68, 'Woodman, Spare that Tree' from L. Shepherd: *The History of Street Literature* (David & Charles, 1973); p. 69, 'Twas in that Garden' from M. Willson Disher: *Victorian Song* (Phoenix House, 1955); p. 69, 'The Wolf' from ibid.; p. 70, 'The Maniac' from ibid.; p. 70, 'The Storm' from ibid.; p. 71, 'Poor Jack' from ibid.; p. 72, 'Father, Dear Father, Come Home' from ibid.; pp. 72–3, 'Ben Battle' from C. Chilton: *Victorian Folk Songs* (Essex, 1965); p. 75, 'Jump Jim Crow' from I. W. Ford: *Traditional Music of America* (Hatsboro Folk Association,

1965); p. 94, 'Martha Gunn' from M. Willson Disher, op. cit.; pp. 94–6, 'The Husbands' Boat' from ibid.; pp. 96–8, 'Wotcher Ria' from J. M. Garrett: *Sixty Years of British Music Hall* (Chappell, 1976); pp. 103–4, 'My Old Dutch' from M. Vicinus, op. cit.

**Quotations**  P. 20, John Pinkerton from C. Pearl: *Bawdy Burns* (Frederick Muller, 1958); pp. 21–2, Alexander Carmichael from F. Collinson: *The Traditional and National Music of Scotland* (RKP, 1966); pp. 22–4, Welsh quotations from W. S. Gwynn Williams: *Welsh National Music and Dance* (Curwen, 1933); p. 29, The Antiquaries of Newcastle from C. Sharp: *English Folk Song: Some Conclusions* (Novello, 1936); p. 30, Lucy Broadwood from M. Karpeles: *An Introduction to English Folk Song* (OUP, 1978); p. 40 the Fraternity of Minstrels from R. Nettel: *Seven Centuries of Popular Song* (Phoenix House, 1956); pp. 40–1, the waits and also the minstrels from J. C. Bridge: *Town Waits and their Tunes* (Proceedings of the Royal Musical Association, 1928); pp. 41–2, Dr Burney from ibid.; p. 44, the *Spectator* from R. Nettel, op. cit.; p. 44, Sir John Etherege from ibid.; p. 45, Ann Barwick from ibid.; p. 45, Norwich waits from J. C. Bridge, op cit.; p. 46, John Banister from A. R. Warwick, op. cit.; p. 52, Sir Hubert Parry from R. Nettel: *Music of the Five Towns* (CUP, 1944); p. 52, jazz values from *Youth Makes Music* (National Council of Social Service, 1957); p. 53, Dr Burney from J. C. Bridge, op. cit.; p. 63, the *Standard* from C. Pulling: *They Were Singing* (Harrap, 1952); p. 63, Mr and Mrs German Reed from ibid.; p. 65, Charles Dibdin from Percy Scholes: *Oxford Companion to Music* (OUP, 1970); p. 67, the lady harpists from ibid.; p. 68, Henry Russell story from S. Spaeth: *A History of Popular Music* (Phoenix House, 1948); p. 78, Stephen Foster from ibid.; pp. 78–9, the Squire from F. Thompson: *Lark Rise to Candleford* (OUP, 1954); p. 85, Thomas Holcroft from E. D. MacKerness: *A Social History of English Music* (RKP, 1964); p. 86, John Curwen from ibid.; p. 86, John Wesley from W. Douglas: *Religious Church Music in History and Practice* (Faber, 1962); p. 87, Moody and Sankey from P. Scholes, op. cit.; p. 87, the Jubilee Singers from T. Seward: *The Story of the Jubilee Singers* (Hodder & Stoughton, 1876); p. 98, Bessie Bellwood from M. Vicinus, op. cit.; p. 104, Mrs Ormiston Chant from M. Vicinus, op. cit.; pp. 108, 111, descriptions of Marie Lloyd from C. McInnes: *Sweet Saturday Night* (McGibbon & Kee, 1967); p. 120, Philip Stubbes from R. Nettel: *Seven Centuries of Popular Song* (Phoenix House, 1956); p. 121, Richard Baxter from E. C. Cawte: 'The Morris Dance in Hereford, Shropshire and Worcestershire', in *Journal of the English Folk Dance and Song Society* (1963); p. 124, the bourrée from A. F. Franks: *Social Dance* (RKP, 1963); p. 126, Cheltenham Assembly Rooms from P. J. S. Richardson: *The Social Dances of the Nineteenth Century in England* (Herbert Jenkins, 1960); p. 127, Northumbrian dancing masters from H. M. Neville: 'A Corner in the North', quoted in *English Dance and Song*, Spring, 1967; p. 129, the waltz and pp. 129–30, the waltz from A. H. Franks, op. cit.; p. 130, Richard Wagner and Heinrich Laube from J. Wechsberg: *The Waltz Emperors* (Weidenfeld & Nicolson, 1973).

**Pictures** Pp. 7, 23, 26, 60, 65, 66, 74, 80, 81, 88, 92, 97, 99, 100, 102, 105, 109, 110, 115, 126 the Radio Times Hulton Picture Library; pp. 12, 13, 123, Geoff Gomme; pp. 77, 95, 119, the Mansell Collection; pp. 4, 57, 62, the Museum of London; pp. 3, 39, Peter Newark's Historical Picture Service; p. 27, Peter Newark's Western Americana Picture Library; p. 122, the English Folk Dance and Song Society; p. 21, the Scottish Tourist Board; p. 18, Claddagh Records, Dublin; p. viii, Sir John Soane's Museum; p. 51, the Royal Philharmonic Orchestra; p. 32, Alan Johnson. Author and publishers are grateful to the above for permission to reproduce copyright material.

# Some suggestions for further reading and listening

**Books**    **Folk music**

Two of the best histories of English folksong are also the most readable. They are:

Karpeles, M. (1973), *An Introduction to English Folk Song*, Oxford University Press.

Lloyd, A. L. (1967), *Folk Song in England*, Lawrence & Wishart. (Published in paperback by Paladin, 1975.)

If you wish to learn some English folksongs, a very good first collection is:

Vaughan Williams, R. and Lloyd, A. L. (eds) (1959), *The Penguin Book of English Folk Songs*, Penguin.

**Drawing-room music**

This subject and many other aspects of music in the period are covered fully and pleasantly by:

Pearsall, R. (1973), *Victorian Popular Music*, David & Charles.

Pearsall, R. (1975), *Edwardian Popular Music*, David & Charles.

If you would like to learn some of the songs, try:

Turner, M. (1972), *The Parlour Song Book: A Casquet of Vocal Gems*, Michael Joseph.

The following book is out of print, but is so excellent that it is worth asking at your local library, and at second-hand bookshops:

Willson Disher, M. (1955), *Victorian Song*, Phoenix House.

**Music hall**

A very pleasant and well-illustrated introduction is:
Hudd, R. (1976), *Music Hall*, Eyre Methuen.

If you wish to learn some songs, try:

*60 Old-Time Variety Songs* (1977), EMI Publishing.

The following book is also out of print, but is again well worth looking for:

Willson Disher, M. (1938), *Winkles and Champagne*,
    Cedric Chivers.

**Recordings**    **Folk music**

Topic Records issue a wide and excellent range of traditional folk music. You should ask to see their catalogue at your local record shop. Just three of their many useful introductions to English folk music are:

*The Iron Muse: A Panorama of Industrial Folk Music*,
    Topic 12T86.
*Songs of Ceremony*, Topic 12T197.
*Sea Songs and Shanties*, TPS 205.

For a total contrast, try

*Music from the Western Isles*, Tangent, TNGM 110.

**Victorian music**

The availability of Victorian material varies; it is therefore best to enquire at record shops and record libraries for the latest releases. But at the time of writing, the following make a useful start:

*Middle-class music*
*The Parlour Song Book* (goes with the book of that
    name), CAS 1078.
*Victorian Ballads*, SHE 208.
*Musical Comedy's Golden Days* (includes tunes from *The
    Geisha*), ABK 12.

*Music hall*
Original recordings can be heard on:

*The Golden Age of Music Hall* (includes Gus Elen, Marie
    Lloyd), RHA 6014.
*Sir Harry Lauder sings Scottish Songs*, GVC 14.
*Top of the Bill* (includes Florrie Forde, Marie Lloyd,
    Eugene Stratton), SHB 22.

# Index